Using Literacy Strategies to Enhance Social Studies Education in Elementary Classrooms

Using Literacy Strategies to Enhance Social Studies Education in Elementary Classrooms

Kathryn L. Roberts and Kristy A. Brugar

ROWMAN & LITTLEFIELD
Lanham • Boulder • New York • London

Rowman & Littlefield
Bloomsbury Publishing Inc, 1385 Broadway, New York, NY 10018, USA
Bloomsbury Publishing Plc, 50 Bedford Square, London, WC1B 3DP, UK
Bloomsbury Publishing Ireland, 29 Earlsfort Terrace, Dublin 2, D02 AY28, Ireland
www.rowman.com

Copyright © 2025 by Kathryn L. Roberts and Kristy A. Brugar

All rights reserved. No part of this publication may be: i) reproduced or transmitted in any form, electronic or mechanical, including photocopying, recording or by means of any information storage or retrieval system without prior permission in writing from the publishers; or ii) used or reproduced in any way for the training, development or operation of artificial intelligence (AI) technologies, including generative AI technologies. The rights holders expressly reserve this publication from the text and data mining exception as per Article 4(3) of the Digital Single Market Directive (EU) 2019/790.

British Library Cataloguing in Publication Information available

Library of Congress Cataloging-in-Publication Data
Names: Brugar, Kristy A. author | Roberts, Kathryn L. author
Title: Using literacy strategies to enhance social studies education in elementary classrooms / Kristy A. Brugar and Kathryn L. Roberts.
Description: Lanham, Maryland : Rowman ; Littlefield, [2025] | Includes bibliographical references and index.
Identifiers: LCCN 2024047766 (print) | LCCN 2024047767 (ebook) | ISBN 9781538197370 cloth | ISBN 9781538197387 paperback | ISBN 9781538197394 ebook
Subjects: LCSH: Social sciences--Study and teaching (Elementary)--United States | Literacy--Study and teaching (Elementary)--United States | Interdisciplinary approach in education--United States | Learning strategies--United States
Classification: LCC LB1584 .B75 2025 (print) | LCC LB1584 (ebook) | DDC 372.89--dc23/eng/20250206
LC record available at https://lccn.loc.gov/2024047766
LC ebook record available at https://lccn.loc.gov/2024047767

For product safety related questions contact productsafety@bloomsbury.com.

∞™ The paper used in this publication meets the minimum requirements of American National Standard for Information Sciences—Permanence of Paper for Printed Library Materials, ANSI/NISO Z39.48-1992.

Contents

Acknowledgments		vii
1	Introduction	1
2	Reading: Summarizing and Synthesizing Sources	9
3	Writing: Writing to Learn and Learning to Write	31
4	Speaking: Developing Argument and Explanation	47
5	Listening: Setting a Purpose, Staying Engaged	67
6	Creating: Multimodal Composition	85
7	Viewing: Interpreting Graphical Sources	103
8	Engaging in Inquiry: Putting It All Together	123
9	Final Thoughts	145
Index		147
About the Authors		155

Acknowledgments

This book was born out of our love for the curious, brilliant students we have had the honor of teaching. Without exception, every practice in this book is grounded in research but also in our own experiences working with students and experiencing the sheer joy of watching them learn with the kind of enthusiasm we wish we could bottle. For this, we owe a debt of gratitude to the students and colleagues we have had the privilege of working with at MSD of Decatur Township, Cranbrook Schools, Elliot Mills Middle School, Michigan State University, Wayne State University, and the University of Oklahoma.

We are also grateful for the support of our families, who granted us grace while we periodically stepped out of their worlds and into the world of writing. This book would not have been possible without the support of John, Brian, Lola, and Jude. We would be remiss in our acknowledgments if we left out our furrier family members, Arlo, Fern, and Finn, who listened to endless meetings and readings of drafts with rapt attention and put in many miles with us as we walked or ran to clarify our thinking. We are less thankful for the time one of those runs included a skunk.

There are also so many people who helped us bring this book from our imaginations into reality. Many thanks to Nathan Davidson and Hollis Peterson at Rowman & Littlefield for their reading of drafts, feedback, and guidance. We are also grateful for the reviewers who gave us valuable feedback along the way. Their reviews were blind, so we cannot thank them individually here, but we hope they see this and know we appreciate them. We also owe a heartfelt thank-you to Kamrin Ratcliff for her editorial assistance.

Finally, to educators: thank you to all of you we have met, haven't met, and hope to meet. You don't get the appreciation you deserve, but we are appreciative of you and all the care you put into teaching every day. We hope this book sparks your curiosity and continues to fuel the vitally important work you do with students and for community. We are grateful for the work you have done and will do toward a better tomorrow.

Kathryn L. Roberts
Kristy A. Brugar

CHAPTER 1

Introduction

"Teaching and learning are interdisciplinary!" "All teachers are teachers of literacy!" If you teach in the elementary grades, you've probably heard or read these statements, or something like them, hundreds of times. You are not alone if you found them frustrating because sure, they make sense, but *how* are content areas supposed to be integrated?

Using a book that is thematically related to a social studies topic in literacy instruction sells social studies instruction (way, way) short. Asking students to use literacy skills in social studies lessons isn't the same as the teaching and learning of content-area literacy. Interdisciplinary instruction requires much more meaningful integration (Hinde, 2015). The purpose of this book is to explicitly present commonly taught social studies content and literacy skills in ways that are interdisciplinary and that forward social studies and literacy learning as well as to provide classroom examples of this work in action.

Integrating literacy and social studies instruction is essential because many of the literacy skills used in social studies are unique to the subject area. In the elementary grades, students are taught to engage in literacy practices, such as reading for understanding, outside of the social studies; but how that is done when reading narrative or informational text is different from how it is done when reading primary or secondary sources, such as maps, letters, captioned images, or timelines, with a particular purpose in mind. If students are being asked to use literacy skills to facilitate social studies learning, they need to be taught how to use those skills in content-area contexts.

So, how does one integrate social studies and literacy teaching and learning in meaningful ways? There is no one answer to that question, but, in this book, we set out to provide you with examples of what it can look like when done well. Specifically, we provide research-based methods for teaching elementary students to use literacy in disciplinary-specific ways to grow their social studies and literacy skills and knowledge. Before we get to that, please humor us and take a brief detour so that we can all get on the same page of what we're talking about when we say "social studies" and "literacy."

What Is Social Studies?

The National Council for the Social Studies (NCSS) broadly defines social studies at the elementary level as "the study of individuals, communities, systems, and their interactions across time and place that prepares students for local, national, and global civic life" (2023, n.p.). When defining social studies at the elementary level, the NCSS also includes "the interdisciplinary study of history, geography, economics, and government/civics and is well-integrated with the study of language arts, the visual and performing arts, and STEM" (n.p.).

Over the last decade, social studies education/educators have been particularly attentive to inquiry-based practices (NCSS, 2013; Swan et al., 2015) in order to meet the goals inherent in the definition of social studies. Most basically, inquiry is the act of asking and answering questions, typically with the goal of sharing the answers with an authentic audience or taking some sort of action. A key feature of inquiry is that questions posed can be answered in many different ways, depending on the person asking the questions, their perspectives or points of view, and the evidence or sources explored. (More information on inquiry can be found in Chapter 8.)

Teaching social studies in elementary classrooms is also different from teaching social studies or any of the individual social studies disciplines at the middle or high school level due to the way that elementary days are typically structured. Because the day is not typically as rigidly scheduled into individual class periods, elementary teachers are often better able to integrate content areas, such as social studies and English language arts. Of course, this also means that there is often no protected time for social studies (Whitlock & Brugar, 2019). That, in combination with social studies not being a focal point for high-stakes testing, can lead to it being deprioritized.

Both understanding what social studies is and understanding why we use our limited time to teach it are important. For over thirty years, the marginalization of social studies has been well documented (Halvorsen, 2013; Houser, 1995; Fitchett & Haefner, 2010). This marginalization has led practitioners, teachers, educators, and educational researchers to think critically about ways in which social studies is present (or not) in elementary classrooms (e.g., Brugar & Whitlock, 2020). It is common to see the integration of social studies with English or language arts in elementary classrooms (Hinde, 2015).

Just so we're all starting on the same figurative page—we need to teach social studies. We can marginalize rote memorization of capitals and state abbreviations, but, when we're talking about social studies as a mechanism to help students examine vast human experiences through the generation of questions, collection and analysis of evidence from credible sources, consideration of multiple perspectives, and application of social studies knowledge and disciplinary skills (NCSS, 2023), we need to teach that. Examining the past, participating in the present, and shaping the future prepares learners for lifelong civic engagement, and that is important.

Social studies centers knowledge of human rights and local, national, and global responsibilities so that learners can work together to create a just world in which they want to live. At the risk of sounding hyperbolic, engaging in such study is literally life changing. We will be the first to admit we are a bit biased in our love of social studies (so much so that we're writing a book about it). However, from this description, it is clear that social studies is not about memorizing capital cities or coloring maps; it is about becoming someone who can fully contribute to and benefit from society, which is objectively important.

What Is Literacy? (Or, More Accurately, What Are Literacies?)

Defining literacy is no easy feat because the term encompasses quite a bit. First, note that we use the term "literacy" and not "reading." Literacy goes far beyond reading (and certainly beyond decoding or "sounding out" words). Second, the definition has evolved and continues to evolve. In 2016, in an article appropriately titled "From 'What Is Reading?' to What Is Literacy?" Katherine Frankel and colleagues defined literacy as "the process of using reading, writing, and oral language to extract, construct, integrate, and critique meaning through interaction and involvement with multimodal texts in the context of socially situated practices" (p. 7).

Frankel and colleagues limited their definition to reading, writing, speaking, and listening but understood those constructs as being relevant to multimodal texts, which includes things such as images, videos, graphical information (e.g., tables, maps), et cetera. In our conceptualization of literacy, we also assume that the word "text" includes multimodal text. However, because the skills required to view ("read") and create ("write") various elements of text are so different from the skills required to read and write purely verbal text, we add viewing and creating to our definition as separate constructs, in addition to reading, writing, listening, and speaking.

A literate person is able to flexibly use skills within each of these six constructs for a variety of purposes, including entertainment, sharing information, requesting information, constructing meaning, critically considering or creating media, understanding various points of view, defending a position, and many, many more. Like social studies, literacy serves a greater purpose than simply enabling reading and writing. Literacy is a gateway to successfully "being" in an increasingly multimodal world.

Finally, "literacy" is actually "literacies" because literacy practices shift to be used in specialized ways in different contexts. There are a variety of terms to help one consider literacy in relation to social studies. These terms include, but are not limited to, ecological literacy (Payne, 2005; Risser, 1986), historical literacy (Nokes, 2012), media literacy (NCSS, 2022), and racial literacy (King, 2022). Throughout this text, we will share examples of how various literacies are used to further students' social studies knowledge and understandings, with particular attention to multimodal literacy, content and disciplinary literacy, and visual literacy.

Multimodal literacy entails readers creating and extracting meaning through a combination of two or more modes of text. For example, a poster may convey meaning through a combination of written language, still images, and spatial design. In a picture book, the print and images contribute to the story, both individually and in coordination. In both examples, each mode has specific functions and readers must make meaning both within and across modalities (e.g., Kress, 2003). In addition, dual-coding theory (Paivio, 1991) suggests that processing information through multiple modes improves memory and comprehension of ideas.

Content-area literacy and disciplinary literacy are related, but distinct, terms. Content-area literacy is the ability to use literacy skills and strategies to create and obtain new information in and across broad content areas, such as social studies, math, and science (McKenna & Robinson, 1993). McKenna and Robinson (1993) identify three components of content-area literacy: general literacy skills, content-specific literacy skills, and prior knowledge of content. Similarly, Swafford and Kallus (2002) extend this definition to include use of background and prior knowledge.

As opposed to focusing on literacy in a broad content area, disciplinary literacy focuses on specialized skills and strategies used in individual disciplines (e.g., civics, history, economics, geography). Disciplinary literacy helps students understand, for example, that historians require different literacy skills and knowledge than geographers (Moje, 2007). Wineburg (2003) argues that historians follow a disciplinary process of reading and analyzing historical narratives, which requires skills such as determining authorship and context. In contrast, geographers are interested in the role of place and may view or create maps to analyze for geopolitical relationships.

Visual literacy is the ability "to interpret, recognize, appreciate, and understand information presented through visible actions, objects, and symbols, natural or man-made" (Institute of Museum and Library Services, n.d., n.p.). In the case of social studies, this often includes fine art, graphs, maps, and photographs. Visual literacy requires constructing meaning with imagery. It involves a set of skills ranging from simple identification (e.g., naming what one sees) to complex interpretation and integration of information (e.g., considering what a table showing population counts and a map showing climate mean when taken together).

Visual literacy calls upon "many aspects of cognition, such as personal association, questioning, speculating, analyzing, fact-finding, and categorizing" (Yenawine, 2004, p. 47). Coincidentally, social studies calls for many of the same aspects of cognition.

Roadmap: How to Use This Book

Social studies concepts offer a literal and figurative world of possibilities to explore with young students. In this book, we explore the instructional relationship between social studies and literacy that allows students to make the most of their time in those worlds. Each chapter aligns with one primary literacy domain—reading, writing, speaking, listening, creating, or viewing—and describes how skills and strategies within that domain can be used to more deeply explore social studies concepts, sources, and critical questions.

Chapter 2 through Chapter 7 can be read in any order. Chapter 8 is designed to show how the constructs, skills, and strategies highlighted in Chapter 2 through Chapter 7 can be combined in classroom inquiries and is best read after reading Chapter 2 through Chapter 7. In each chapter, you will find an introductory vignette; a bit of background on the literacy construct; research-based pedagogical examples to effectively introduce, support, and assess social studies with attention to literacy skills; ideas for additional resources; and exemplar lesson ideas for each grades K–2 and 3–5. You'll also find a short list of "chat and change" questions that are helpful if you're discussing the book with colleagues.

The lesson ideas are brief descriptions of instructional strategies that can be used to teach social studies content (i.e., civics, economics, geography, history) at a particular grade level. While they are framed around specific content for the purpose of illustration, in all cases the content can be changed to topics appropriate to individual classroom contexts (i.e., grade level, content, specific student support needs). Our intention is not to create a script to follow, although we do share illustrative language (noted in italics in each lesson). Rather, the lessons serve as frameworks or guides that can be adapted to your particular students and classroom.

The lesson ideas in this book are meant to give readers an idea of what leveraging literacy instruction within social studies instruction can look like in both the primary and intermediate grades. They are designed to give students the tools they need for deep, critical engagement with social studies content. From there, the expectation is that students will be supported to use those tools to draw their own conclusions, build their own knowledge, and ask their own questions.

The exemplar lessons are written to be appropriate for the grade band, not a particular grade, and for a wide range of students. We've not had the opportunity to meet your students, though we wish we could. What this means, in practical terms, is that it is up to those who know the students best—their teachers—to tailor the lessons to students' strengths and needs. This may include integrating supports from students' individualized education programs (IEPs) and 504 plans, adding language goals, changing out materials to make them more or less challenging, changing out materials to build on what students have already learned, and modifying assessments.

Before we close this chapter, we offer a note on everyone's favorite topic: standards. This book is meant to be useful and realistic; part of being realistic is understanding that teachers are obligated to teach standards. However, linking every lesson to the social studies and English language arts standards for every state would get a bit unwieldy. For this reason, we ground our lessons in two anchor documents, *The College, Career, and Civic Life (C3) Framework for Social Studies State Standards: Guidance for Enhancing the Rigor of K–12 Civics, Economics, Geography, and History* (*C3 Framework*; NCSS, 2013) and the *Common Core State Standards for English Language Arts* (National Governors Association Center for Best Practices and Council of Chief State School Officers, 2010).

The *C3 Framework* has been used by most states as a framework for creating state social studies standards, with attention to both content knowledge and skills, particularly those related to inquiry. If you're not familiar with the *C3 Framework*, it is worth browsing and is free! (See the References for the link.) You'll probably recognize a lot of the content from your own state standards. Similarly, state literacy standards are identical to, adapted from, or closely mirror the state literacy standards (National Governors Association Center for Best Practices and Council of Chief State School Officers, 2010).

While the indicators and standards listed in the lessons do not reflect the standards of individual states, in most cases they closely parallel grade-level social studies and English language arts standards; aligning them to individual state standards should not be difficult. Generally, this means that the lesson ideas in this book are appropriate for your curriculum and classroom and already align or can be easily aligned to your state standards.

On that happy note, it is time to choose your own adventure. There is no one right way to read this book, so dive into whatever chapter captures your interest and enjoy!

Chat and Change

"Chat and change" topics can be used as a menu of discussion starters for professional learning communities (PLCs), teacher education courses, or book clubs. You can also use them to guide your individual thinking about how to move the instructional practices in the chapter into your classroom. As you begin to explore and read, think about the following questions:

- How do you currently teach social studies? What is the role of social studies in your classroom?
- What skills do your students need to be able to engage in social studies learning with increasing independence?
- In what ways do you integrate social studies and literacy?
- What sources do you use or aspire to use in your social studies instruction?
- What are your hopes for your students as citizens and members of communities?

References

Brugar, K. A., & Whitlock, A. M. (2020). Explicit and implicit social studies: Exploring the integration of social studies experiences in two elementary classrooms. *Canadian Social Studies, 51*(2), 2–21.

Fitchett, P. G., & Heafner, T. L. (2010). A national perspective on the effects of high-stakes testing and standardization on elementary social studies marginalization. *Theory & Research in Social Education, 38*(1), 114–130.

Frankel, K. K., Becker, B. L. C., Rowe, M. W., & Pearson, P. D. (2016). From "what is reading?" to what is literacy? *Journal of Education, 196*(3), 7–17.

Halvorsen, A. (2013). *A history of elementary social studies: Romance and reality.* Peter Lange.

Hinde, E. (2015). The theoretical foundations of curriculum integration and its application to social studies instruction. In L. Bennett & E. R. Hinde (Eds.), *Becoming integrated thinkers: Case studies in elementary social studies* (pp. 21–29). National Council for the Social Studies.

Houser, N. (1995). Social studies on the back burner: Views from the field. *Theory and Research in Social Education, 23*(2), 147–168.

Institute of Museum and Library Services. (n.d.). *Museums, libraries, and 21st century skills: Definitions*. Institute of Museum and Library Services. https://www.imls.gov/issues/national-initiatives/museums-libraries-and-21st-century-skills/definitions

King, L. G. (2022). *Racial literacies and social studies: Curriculum, instruction, and learning*. Teachers College Press.

Kress, G. (2003). *Literacy in the new media age* (pp. 35–59). Routledge.

McKenna, M. C., & Robinson, R. D. (1993). Content literacy: A definition and implications. *Journal of Reading, (34)*3, 184–186.

Moje, E. B. (2007). Developing socially just subject-matter instruction: A review of the literature on disciplinary literacy teaching. *Review of Research in Education, 31*(1), 1–44.

National Council for the Social Studies. (2013). *The college, career, and civic life (C3) framework for social studies state standards: Guidance for enhancing the rigor of K–12 civics, economics, geography, and history*. Authors. https://www.socialstudies.org/sites/default/files/c3/C3-Framework-for-Social-Studies.pdf.

National Council for the Social Studies. (2022). *Media literacy*. National Council for the Social Studies. https://www.socialstudies.org/position-statements/media-literacy

National Council for the Social Studies. (2023). *About the National Council for the Social Studies*. National Council for the Social Studies. https://www.socialstudies.org/about

National Governors Association Center for Best Practices, & Council of Chief State School Officers. (2010). *Common core state standards*. Authors. https://www.thecorestandards.org/ELA-Literacy/

Nokes, J. (2012). *Building students' historical literacies: Learning to read and reason with historical texts and evidence*. Routledge.

Paivio, A. (1991). Dual coding theory: Retrospect and current status. *Canadian Journal of Psychology, 45*(3), 255–287.

Payne, P. (2005). Lifeworld and textualism: Reassembling the research/ed and "others." *Environmental Education Research, 11*, 413–431.

Risser, P. G. (1986). Ecological literacy. *Bulletin of the Ecological Society of America, 67*, 264–270.

Swafford, J., & Kallus, M. (2002). Content literacy: A journey into the past, present and future. *Journal of Content Area Reading, 1*(1), 7–18.

Swan, K., Lee, J., & Grant, S. G. (2015). The New York State toolkit and the inquiry design model: Anatomy of an inquiry. *Social Education, 79*(5), 316–322.

Whitlock, A. M., & Brugar, K. A. (2019). "Snack time" social studies: Observations of social studies instruction in unstructured spaces. *Journal of Social Studies Research, 43*(3), 229–239.

Wineburg, S. S. (2003). Teaching the mind good habits. *The Chronicle of Higher Education, B2*.

Yenawine, P. (2004). Thoughts on visual literacy essay. In J. Flood, S. B. Heath, & D. Lapp (Eds.), *Handbook of research on teaching literacy through the communicative and visual arts*. Routledge.

CHAPTER 2

Reading

SUMMARIZING AND SYNTHESIZING SOURCES

The fifth-grade students are gathered in small groups around the room, with stacks of books among them. Their teacher, Mr. D, says, "Over the next two weeks, you will be meeting in these groups and reading the books in the center of your tables. Sometimes you will read and talk together and sometimes, like today, you will read independently and then talk about what you have read with your classmates. Before we start reading, I think it is really important that we all know a little about the books that are available to us so everyone can select something they would like to read."

The children look from Mr. D to one another with curiosity and anticipation. Mr. D continues, "You are going to be able to look at each of the books at the center of your table. So, when I say "go," you will each take one of the books from the center of your table. I will set the timer and, for five minutes, you are going to skim the book to get an idea of what it is about. What does it mean when we skim a book?" Hands go up across the classroom, and students share lots of different things they might do when skimming. Mr. D. reminds them to check the anchor chart, which has several options noted:

- *Read the title to activate or build background knowledge.*
- *Look at the pictures or people in the pictures, and read captions.*
- *Read any maps, timelines, graphs, and tables that are in your text.*
- *Notice vocabulary words or boldface text.*
- *Read or look at insets and fact boxes.*
- *Read the sidebars.*
- *Read the first and last paragraphs or the topic sentence of each paragraph.*

Mr. D continues, "After five minutes, I am going to ask you to record some of the things you find out on this graphic organizer (Appendix A). Then, I am going to ask you to repeat this process with another book. We are going to do this five times. Does anyone have any questions?" One student asks, "Isn't this a book pass, Mr. D? I think we did this before to look at lots of books." Mr. D. responds, "You are absolutely right! This is a book pass, and we have done it before."

The students ready their hands to grab one of the books from the stack. Mr. D says, "Oh, and one more thing—all of these books have something in common. I will ask you

Written in Bone (2009)

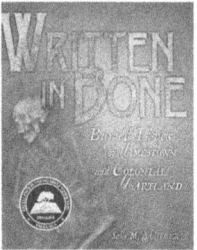

Blizzard of Glass (2011)

Frozen Secrets: Antarctica Revealed (2013)

Deadly Aim: The Civil War Story of Michigan's Anishinaabe Sharpshooters (2019)

Underground Fire: Hope, Sacrifice, and Courage in the Cherry Mine Disaster (2022)

Figure 2.1.   Books by Sally M. Walker.

what you think the commonality might be when we are in a whole group again, so be thinking about that as you skim. Let's begin!" After grabbing their books, students immediately engage and react to the texts. Phrases like "Wow!"; "Look at this!"; and "I didn't know that!" are heard throughout the room.

After almost thirty minutes, the students have skimmed five books: *Written in Bone; Blizzard of Glass; Underground Fire: Hope, Sacrifice, and Courage in the Cherry Mine Disaster; Deadly Aim: The Civil War Story of Michigan's Anishinaabe Sharpshooters;* and *Frozen Secrets: Antarctica Revealed.* (See Figure 2.1.) In each of these texts, Sally M. Walker dives into a little-known history through a use of historical, archeological, and scientific evidence. The use of this evidence is an integral aspect of each book.

The class settles back in as a whole group, and Mr. D begins their discussion with, "Did anyone learn anything interesting?" Students share interesting facts about archeology, explosions, the Civil War, and explorers—all topics of the books they explored. He continues by asking, "So, what do these books have in common?" The students pause before accurately sharing, "These are all true stories," "These are nonfiction," and "The same person wrote ALL five books!"

This vignette illustrates the use of a "book pass." All too often, students (K–12 and beyond) make book selections without considering the range of materials available. A book pass provides students opportunities to explore a wide range of books in a short period of time in order to make more careful and educated choices—considering their interests, purposes for reading, and the difficulty of the text.

In addition, the book pass provides quick exposure to a range of information on an issue as well as to potentially differing perspectives on a particular author or a specific historical event. Further, the book pass provides students with access to lots of books and provides opportunities for teachers to support students in practicing strategies for quickly skimming a book. For the purpose of teaching social studies, this strategy can be adapted to preview a wide range of primary and secondary source materials, in addition to books.

What Is Reading?

When we refer to reading in this chapter (and book), what we are talking about is reading comprehension, or the ability to construct meaning with and extract meaning from texts in all of their modalities (e.g., RAND, 2002). We also acknowledge that reading is complicated, involving a multitude of factors—a fact that scientific research on reading is very clear on (e.g., Cervetti et al., 2020; Cutting et al., 2015; Duke & Cartwright, 2021; Scarborough, 2001). In order to be effective teachers of reading, educators must have these important foundational understandings.

As illustrated in Figure 2.2, reading is influenced by text, task, sociocultural context, and a multitude of reader factors. While decoding ability is one (very important) factor, the Active View of Reading (Duke & Cartwright, 2021), based on decades of empirical research, makes it abundantly clear that many other factors also contribute to reading. The model also highlights areas in which content may deeply influence reading, such as vocabulary, background knowledge, content knowledge, and motivation

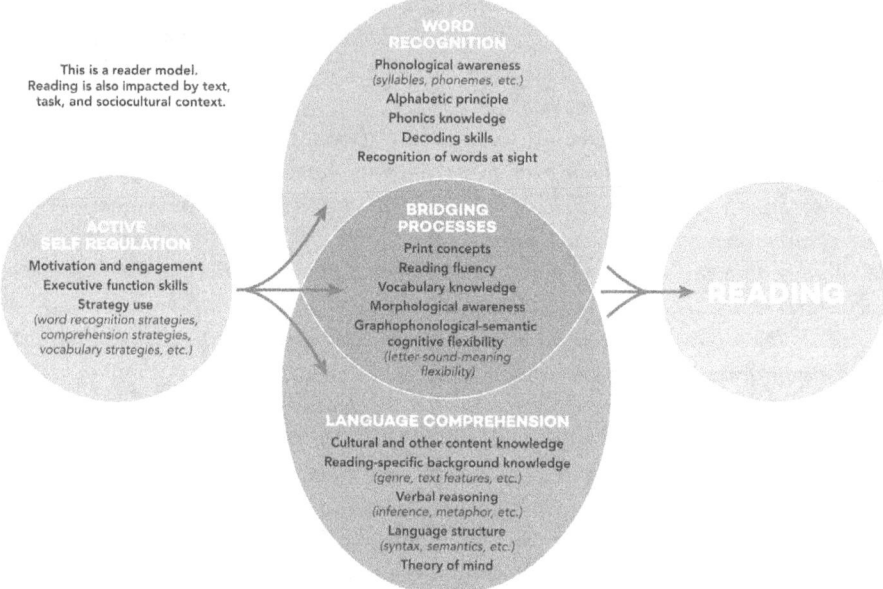

Figure 2.2. Active View of Reading (Duke & Cartwright, 2021, p. 33). Reprinted from "The science of reading progresses: Communicating advances beyond the Simple View of Reading," by N. K. Duke and K. B. Cartwright, 2021, Reading Research Quarterly, 56(S1), S25-S44. Copyright 2021. Authors. Reprinted with permission. Note. Several wordings in this model are adapted from Scarborough (2001).

and engagement. In the context of social studies, this means there are many opportunities to lean on student strengths and build up areas of need.

WHY IS READING IMPORTANT?

Reading is an important mechanism through which we are able to take in information and build understanding. A central goal of reading instruction is to create independent readers, which is essential if students and citizens are to consider information from various sources, many of which are written texts or multimodal texts that contain written language. Many of the goals of social studies, as well as informed citizenry, hinge upon reading. Collaboratively and independently gathering information from a variety of sources, making evidence-based claims, and investigating multiple perspectives are prerequisites for meeting such goals (National Council for the Social Studies, 2013).

Reading both builds and is dependent upon content knowledge. Deeper understanding of content supports reading comprehension of new, related content (e.g., Cabell & Hwang, 2020). This can be tricky in social studies as many sources that students work with, particularly primary sources, assume cultural and content knowledge that students may not have because students were not the original intended audience. It is not surprising, then, that teachers' intentional building of students' background knowledge positively impacts reading abilities within related texts (e.g., Cabell & Hwang, 2020).

Recognizing the role of background knowledge can also help teachers think about their students not as being "strong" or "struggling" readers, but rather think about reading ability as being context dependent. Readers who excel in reading during language arts may have considerable difficulty and need additional support in reading some social studies texts for which they have little background knowledge. Conversely, readers who typically have difficulty in reading during language arts may excel at reading texts for which they have a great deal of background knowledge.

Pedagogies for Reading

The Active View of Reading (Duke & Cartwright, 2021), described above, makes it quite clear that good reading is, well, active. Passive decoding of the words is not enough to build strong reading comprehension under any circumstances and certainly not when children are being asked to engage in the types of critical consideration of texts called for in the social studies.

One way in which students learn to be active readers is by learning to be strategic readers. Reading strategies are "deliberate, goal-directed attempts to control and modify the reader's efforts to decode text, understand words, and construct meanings of text" (Afflerbach et al., 2008, p. 368). Research indicates that, when children are explicitly taught strategies and how to use them, scaffolded to use them, and then supported as they do so with increasing independence, it improves their reading comprehension.

Importantly, learning to use reading strategies improves reading comprehension, not only for older and more proficient readers, but also for very young readers and children who have learning disabilities (e.g., Berkeley et al., 2010; Okkinga et al., 2018; Shanahan et al., 2010). The powerful impact of comprehension instruction again pushes back on the idea that there are inherently "strong" and "struggling" readers and, rather, reframes our thinking so that we can consider readers who need more and less support to deliberately control and monitor their own reading outcomes.

There are many effective strategies that students can be taught, such as summarizing, making inferences, asking and answering questions, activating and using prior knowledge, using text structure, retelling, skimming or scanning text, identifying main ideas and key details, and creating mental images. Each of these strategies can be explicitly taught, modeled, scaffolded, and supported in context. In this chapter, we look closely at two strategies: asking and answering questions and previewing text by skimming and scanning.

When readers ask themselves questions while reading (i.e., self-questioning), it improves their comprehension of the text and topic (e.g., Joseph et al., 2016; Taboada & Guthrie, 2006). Self-questioning helps students monitor comprehension before, during, and after reading, likely because questions focus readers' attention on the most important information in the text. Of course, what is most important depends on the purpose for reading, which is often determined by a reader's question. Strategically reading for particular information has strong, positive effects on reading comprehension (e.g., Murphy et al., 2009).

Answering questions is also a valuable inquiry skill; however, using (reputable) sources to answer questions is a skill that requires instruction. Sometimes, students have prior knowledge that helps them answer a question, and they need to locate information in texts to confirm, refine, or expand their responses. Other times, students are using the texts to locate new information. Helping students understand that information used to answer questions may come from their own prior knowledge, the text, or a combination is a powerful way to help them read strategically and verify their learning (e.g., Raphael, 1984; Raphael & Au, 2005).

The second strategy, previewing text by skimming and scanning, allows students to preview text to make quick determinations about the content and fit for the reading purpose. Pressley and Afflerbach (1996), in their analysis of verbal protocols, determined that strong readers briefly preview texts and have a fairly good idea of what they are about before they even begin reading. Readers might get the basic gist of a text by skimming a section of or the whole text or by scanning to locate particular information. Both processes are done relatively quickly, with the intent of reading the text or text excerpts more carefully if they fit the reader's purpose.

Skimming gives readers a broad preview of the text, provided that it is not done haphazardly. Readers are typically taught to look at certain elements so that skimming is systematic. For example, Abdelrahman and Bsharah (2014) recommend that, for each paragraph, readers read the first sentence, last sentence, and key words in between. Skilled readers also monitor their skimming, attending to when they may need to slow down and read more carefully (e.g., Coiro & Dobler, 2007).

When skilled readers scan for particular information, they may attend to labels, headings and subheadings, bolded words, images, hyperlinks, or particular phrases (e.g., Coiro & Dobler, 2007). Effective scanning also requires monitoring, both to determine whether the text at hand contains the desired information and to make sure the reader stays focused on what they are looking for.

CLASSROOM APPLICATIONS, K–2

A very important premise for teaching reading strategies to young children, particularly in the context of content learning, is that young children are capable of and interested in learning from what they read and what is read to them. They do not have to wait until they are fully proficient readers to learn from text (e.g., Wright, 2018–2019), and, if we ask them to wait for years to use their reading skills for meaningful and interesting purposes, persisting in reading instruction through those early years is going to be a slow and tedious slog for everyone involved.

CONNECTIONS TO THE *C3 FRAMEWORK* AND *COMMON CORE STATE STANDARDS*

The *C3 Framework* refers to the need to read critically within each discipline in several places. However, many of the individual indicators also inherently require reading, even if this is not stated explicitly. For example, students are asked to analyze sources, many of which are written or include some written information. They are also asked to describe, evaluate, explain, identify, et cetera. While these tasks might involve many skills, in most cases the information can be found, at least in part, in something students have read. In this lesson, students compare information stemming largely from historical sources that they read.

Individually and with others, students . . .
D2.His.2.K–2. Compare life in the past to life today.
D2.His.12.K–2. Generate questions about a particular historical source as it relates to a particular historical event or development.

The *Common Core State Standards for English Arts* contain a plethora of standards related to reading, focused on both code-based and meaning-based skills and knowledge. In the social studies, the primary focus is on meaning-based reading skills and knowledge. While the sources students read during social studies instruction can be of any genre, in this lesson the focus is primarily on informational text.

RI.K.1: With prompting and support, ask and answer questions about key details in a text.
RI.1.1: Ask and answer questions about key details in a text.
RI.2.1: Ask and answer such questions as *who*, *what*, *where*, *when*, *why*, and *how* to demonstrate understanding of key details in a text.
RI.1.6: Distinguish between information provided by pictures or other illustrations and information provided by the words in a text.

Reading in Action, K–2

Young children are full of questions. Learning to ask questions that help identify important and interesting information is an important part of learning. Learning to read in focused ways to answer those questions is equally important. As noted above, both are linked to better comprehension.

In the lesson that follows, grades K–2 students approach text through reading—on their own, with assistance, or with technology supports—for the purpose of answering specific questions raised in a previous lesson. The role of the teacher is to teach them a strategy for doing this, model the strategy, and then support children with as much scaffolding as they need as they move toward using it independently. It is important to remember that the gradual release of control is unlikely to happen in one lesson. More likely, it will take months, or sometimes even years, particularly for emergent readers.

The strategy in this lesson is "Question-Answer Relationships" (Raphael, 1984; Raphael & Au, 2005), in which students are guided to think carefully about where the answers to their questions come from and provide evidence. The strategy entails teaching children about two sources of information—the book and their brains—that can be used alone or in combination to answer questions: in the book (right there,

16   CHAPTER 2

think and search) and in my head (on my own, author and me). In this lesson, two of these four options are introduced, right there and author and me, though students may naturally use the other two.

This lesson is a snapshot—just one peek into a classroom in which students have been participating in many other lessons. The lesson itself includes skills and strategies that are not the focal points of the lesson. Students read print and graphics, use assistive technology, and use previously taught classroom norms for working with peers. That definitely does not mean they have mastered these skills and strategies! Scaffolding can be used to bridge the gaps.

1. Introduce the Lesson

This lesson is intended to be taught midway into an inquiry conducted in response to the compelling question, "How have time and technology changed what it is like to live in our community?" This week, the students have been considering the supporting question, "What was it like to live here in the past?" As inquiry often does, the

Figure 2.3. Anchor Chart of Students' Questions About What it was Like to Live in Their Community in the Past.

supporting question led them to ask even more questions, which were recorded on chart paper the day before so as to be visible to the whole class (Figure 2.3).

Prepare for this lesson by curating a selection of texts that students can explore in small groups or pairs. Make sure you have at least two texts that can be used to explore each question. For students who are not yet conventionally reading or not able to access some texts due to difficulty in decoding, text-to-speech technology can be used with online sources, students can be paired with a stronger reader, or the teacher or another adult can sit in with a small group to facilitate. If you're using electronic resources, it is best to have the tabs already pulled up for each group or to provide a document with clickable links.

If students have been taught strategies for viewing and analyzing photos and other images (see Chapter 7 for an example), whether stand-alone or embedded in text, photo collections are a good option. If they have not been taught strategies for this, the photos are still good sources, but their use will likely require more teacher support. Suggestions for resources are provided below.

Sample Texts Used in the K–2 Lesson

Primary Source Collections:

Library of Congress Primary Source Set: Child Labor (select images)
Library of Congress Primary Source Set: Children's Lives at the Turn of the Twentieth Century (select images)

Books:

Communication Then and Now, Robin Nelson (2003 [paperback]; 2018 [Kindle])
Home Then and Now, Robin Nelson (2003 [paperback]; 2018 [Kindle])
If You Traveled West in a Covered Wagon, Ellen Levine (1992)
School Then and Now, Robin Nelson (2003 [paperback]; 2018 [Kindle])
Toys and Games Then and Now, Robin Nelson (2003)
Transportation Then and Now, Robin Nelson (2003 [paperback]; 2018 [Kindle])
Working Then and Now, Robin Nelson (2007)

Books Available with Decoding Assist*:

Cars 100 Years Ago, Allison Lassieur (2011)
Clothes 100 Years Ago, Allison Lassieur (2011)
Food 100 Years Ago, Allison Lassieur (2011)
Phones 100 Years Ago, Allison Lassieur (2011)
School 100 Years Ago, Allison Lassieur (2011)
Communication Then and Now, Bobbie Kalman (2014)
Community Helpers Then and Now, Bobbie Kalman (2014)
Food and Farming Then and Now, Bobbie Kalman (2014)
School Days Then and Now, Bobbie Kalman (2014)
Toys and Games Then and Now, Bobbie Kalman (2014)
Travel Then and Now, Bobbie Kalman (2014)

*Available in print and electronically on Epic.com with decoding assist

We've been working on our inquiry about how technology has changed our community over time. Yesterday, we were thinking about what it would have been like to live in our community fifty or even one hundred years ago. We had a lot of questions about that! [Review the questions posted on the anchor chart.]

Today, we're going to explore some sources that might help us answer our questions. With a partner/small group, you will decide which question you are most curious about, and I will help you identify some sources that might help you answer it.

We will be learning to read for a specific purpose—answering a question—and will *monitor our reading to make sure we find the answer. If you think you might already have some information to answer the question in your head, you can also read to confirm or check your answer. It's important to stay focused on your question—answering it is your purpose for reading. However, while you're doing that, you're probably going to learn a lot of other cool things.*

While we're working, we're going to make note of what we learn, particularly what we learn that can help us answer our questions, and where our information is coming from. We will share that at the end of our reading time.

2. Teach the Lesson Using a Research-Based Instructional Practice (here, Question-Answer Relationships, [Raphael, 1984; Raphael & Au, 2005])

For this part of the lesson, students will need to be in groups of two to four students who are interested in researching the same question. Depending on grouping routines in your classroom, you may do this in advance by letting children choose groups and asking them to choose their topics the day before, using existing groups and letting the groups pick topics, or grouping students in some other strategic way (e.g., ensuring that at least one student in each group knows how to use the text-to-speech and highlighting tools for electronic sources). Grouping the students prior to instruction allows them to select their topics and have those in mind during the whole-group part of the lesson.

Today we're really going to think about where our information comes from. There are lots of sources of information, but today we're going to focus on the information we have in our heads, which is called prior knowledge. Prior means "from before," so prior knowledge is what you know before you start researching. We're also going to focus on information we can find in texts. Those might be books, websites, articles, pictures, graphs, tables—all kinds of things!

Eventually, it will be important to put together all kinds of information from what we already know and texts, but for today we're going to focus on "right there" information. That means you can say, "the answer to the question is right there" and touch it. The questions you have been asking have more than one answer, so you will probably find lots of answers you can touch.

Let's try this out together. I'm going to start with the question, "What kinds of things did kids have?" It's really important to stay focused on my question, so I'm going to take some notes.

[Show the Research Notes Organizer, Appendix B.] *I don't have any group members, so I'm going to leave space up at the top blank. When you get started researching, each person in your group needs to write his or her name here. Next, there is a spot to write my question.* [Model copying the question from the anchor chart to the organizer.] *This is really important because having it right here will help me remember to stay focused—this is what I'm reading to find out.*

I have several texts here—paper books, electronic books, and photographs. A lot of these sources will show or tell me the kinds of things kids in our community had a long time ago. I'm going to look at two sources: this book, Home Then and Now, *and these pictures from the Library of Congress website.* [Show both resources.]

Before I get into my sources, I'm going to stop and think about what I know about what people had in the past. Hmm. I remember seeing a movie where they didn't have many toys. That's a good start, but that tells me what they didn't have, not what they did have. I'm going to keep thinking. Hmm. I think I remember that they also had pets in that movie. I'm not sure that's true, but I'm going to make a note of it right here where it says "What did you learn that helps you answer the question?" so that I remember to check my sources to see if it is true.

Next, I'm going to check this first option, "Prior Knowledge and Right There (in the text)." This reminds me that I think I know this already, but, to be sure, I need to find information in a text that either matches or changes my thinking. I have to do some research before I can be sure. "Right there in the text" means I read, listen to, or look at something in one of these sources that confirms my prior knowledge or tells me that it is correct. If I find something "right there" in writing or in a picture or graphic that confirms my prior knowledge, it means I can touch it. If I find something is "right there," in the words, it means I hear or read something specific answers the question.

These sources have a lot of really interesting stuff in them. That's awesome; we love learning new things! We need to stay focused to answer our questions, but if there is something really cool that you find in one of your sources that you want to learn more about later, you can make note of that, too. [Show students the second page of the organizer, the "Parking Lot."] *If you come across something really interesting that doesn't answer your question, you can put it in the "parking lot." That way, it won't get lost and you can come back to it later. You can mark whether it came from your prior knowledge or text, just like the answers to your question.*

Model browsing a few of the photographs from one of the Library of Congress collections, adding or confirming information and adding one piece of information to the parking lot. Be sure to talk about whether your information confirms prior knowledge. If not, explain that putting the information in the blank box on the far right with the name of the source means it is not yet confirmed.

[When new information is added to the organizer, add the title of the source to the far-right box.] *In this last box, we're going to make note of where the information came from so that we can get back to it to show the rest of the class or to double-check what we learned. For images, we'll write down the title. For paper books and images, we'll write the book title and page number, when there is one. We can also use a sticky note to mark the page. For electronic books, we'll write the title and page number.* [Note that there are other options for "marking" digital pages, such as taking screen shots.]

[Model browsing *Home Then and Now*, adding or confirming information and adding one piece of information to the parking lot. Be sure to talk about whether your information confirms prior knowledge. If not, explain that putting the information in the blank box on the far right with the name of the source means it is not yet confirmed. Mark pages where you find information with a sticky note.] *I wrote down the title and page number for this information, but I'm also going to mark it with a sticky note so I can find it quickly, later. OK. I've looked through two sources and made some good notes. I have some information that helps me answer my question. Also, on the second page of my notes, I have written some ideas of what I might want to learn about next. Now it's your turn! Let's go over what we will be doing in our groups today.*

Explain the steps briefly to students while you write them in a place where students will be able to refer back to them. Alternatively, you can provide paper copies of the directions for each group. The steps should include the following:

1. Write your names at the top of the paper.
2. Choose a question. (Alternatively, "Write your question at the top of the page.")
3. See the teacher for sources to explore.
4. Think about your prior knowledge. If you have an idea or two, write them in the first column. Each idea goes in a separate box.
5. Read, view, or listen to the sources with your small group.
6. Use your graphic organizer to take notes that answer your question (page 1) and that give you new ideas to think about (page 2).
7. Make sure you have information in all three columns, unless you are not able to confirm your prior knowledge.

We're going to work for about thirty minutes. If you need more space to record information, there are extra graphic organizers here. You do not need to repeat writing the names of the group members and the questions if you use more pages; we can staple them together when you're done. At the end of the thirty minutes, we'll come back together and share at least one thing each group learned. When you do that, one person in your group will tell us what your question was, one piece of information that helped you answer it, and where you found the information. You're also going to show us the page or screen where you learned the information.

Give students time to work; circulate to support, as needed. With five minutes remaining, direct them to choose a piece of information to share and to be prepared both to share the information and to show us exactly where it came from. Remind them that they should be able to touch the information. Circulate and ask groups about what they plan to share before pulling the class back together.

3. Provide Closure

When we are reading about a topic, we can learn a lot of things. If we want to answer a particular question, it's helpful for us to keep that question in mind as we read and mark or take notes as we look for information that can help us answer it. When we are answering questions using texts, we aren't guessing. We are looking for evidence. Sometimes that evidence is in a picture or graphic, sometimes it's in the words, and sometimes it's in both places.

While we're trying to answer questions, we will probably come across other interesting stuff. That is fantastic and part of what makes reading so fun. We can mark and hold on to that information, too, because we might want to share it or investigate more. It's a good idea to mark that information in a different way so that you can easily see whether you are also finding information to answer your question, which is your main focus.

Once we learn all of these interesting things, we can share our ideas with others! It is important to share both what we learned and where we learned it so that whoever we are sharing with understands that we did good research and have accurate information. We're going to do that now! [Invite each group to share their question, one thing they learned, and the source of their learning. Prompt as needed to make sure all three items are addressed.]

Resources for Reading: K-2

Teacher Resources for Reading:

Classroom Materials at the Library of Congress: The Library of Congress offers a wide variety of primary source sets that you can search by keyword or browse by topic, era, or recommended grade level. https://www.loc.gov/classroom-materials/

Library of Congress: Finding Primary Sources: Beyond the primary sources offered by the Library of Congress itself, the Library of Congress provides a full guide for finding additional primary sources in the form of curated sets, online collections, and connections with experts. https://www.loc.gov/programs/teachers/getting-started-with-primary-sources/finding/

Classroom Strategies:

Question-Answer Relationship (QAR): This brief article provides information on what the QAR strategy is as well as why and how to use it. It also includes three videos of classroom instruction and classroom resources for implementing the QAR strategy. https://www.readingrockets.org/classroom/classroom-strategies/question-answer-relationship-qar

---

CLASSROOM APPLICATIONS, 3–5

When children are reading to learning, it is essential to forefront the purpose of reading or what they hope to learn from reading a particular text. In addition, noting the genre helps students approach a particular text most effectively.

CONNECTIONS TO THE *C3 FRAMEWORK* AND *COMMON CORE STATE STANDARDS*

As mentioned for the K–2 example, the *C3 Framework* identifies several skills needed for students to read critically. In this lesson, students gather information from a variety of sources in order to organize and compare information.

Individually and with others, students . . .

D1.5.3–5. Determine the kinds of sources that will be helpful in answering compelling and supporting questions, taking into consideration the different opinions people have about how to answer the questions.
D2.His.2.3–5. Compare life in specific historical time periods to life today.

Common Core State Standards for English Arts

RI.3.1. Ask and answer questions to demonstrate understanding of a text, referring explicitly to the text as the basis for the answer.
RI.3.2. Determine the main idea of a text; recount the key details and explain how they support the main idea.

Reading in Action, 3–5

In later elementary grades, students are asked to use a variety of reading materials to respond to teacher-generated prompts as well as their own questions and wonderings. Being able to utilize multiple texts effectively is an essential skill for students to develop as there is limited time in the school day and certainly limited time devoted to elementary social studies (Fitchett & Heafner, 2010).

As with the K–2 lesson, the following lesson is simply a glimpse into classroom instruction. In this lesson, students are developing and utilizing previewing skills to skim and scan informational text for specific information related to a larger unit of study on Indigenous people of the Great Lakes region, specifically, Michigan. While this lesson is focused on state-specific content (because Indigenous groups are regional), the instructional process can be used to explore a wide range of topics. It works particularly well when students are looking to compare the same categories of information across multiple examples within a larger topic, but it can also be used to explore just one example by omitting the end of the lesson when responses are combined (e.g., investigate only the Potawatami).

1. Introduce the Lesson

This state history lesson is taught early in a unit about the Indigenous people of Michigan: notably, the Ojibwa, the Potawatomi, and the Ottawa. The objective of this lesson is to explore the compelling question, "In the past, what was life like for the Indigenous people of Michigan?" In order to explore this question, students examine historical aspects of daily life for these groups of people.

The structure of this lesson can be easily adapted to the study of other regional or national groups (e.g., people of the Eastern Woodlands, the Pacific Northwest, the Southwest, etc.) or topics (e.g., branches of government, the British and the Patriots). The information in the student textbook is somewhat limited, so it is important to access information from other sources and to encourage students to skim and scan for information across various sources.

We have been learning about groups of people who have called the Great Lakes region home for many generations, long before Michigan became a state. Yesterday, we talked about our inquiry question or the topic we are going to explore together. Remember, that question was, "In the past, what was life like for the Indigenous people of Michigan?" Today we are going to read a bit about three specific groups of Indigenous people: the Ojibwa, the Potawatomi, and the Ottawa.

2. Teach the Lesson Using a Research-Based Instructional Practice (Previewing [Graves, Cooke, & LaBerge, 1983]; Skimming and Scanning [Maxwell, 1972])

Previewing is when a reader quickly looks through a text for information related to their purpose for reading. As readers preview a text, they are identifying information but also noting the structure and features of the text. Proficient readers often preview texts before reading more deeply, typically by scanning or skimming part or all of the text. Harmer (2007) described scanning as engaging with text in order to find particular information. In the social studies, students typically scan for names, dates, and locations—in other words, specific facts. When looking for facts on a particular concept, they may also look for keywords (e.g., "resources," "benefits").

Today we are going to be historians investigating the ways in which the Ojibwe, the Potawatomie, and the Ottawa peoples lived in Michigan before Michigan was a state. Does anyone know how long ago that may have been? [Students may share responses or guesses.] *Michigan became a state in 1837. While we are studying life in the past, it is important to remember that the Ojibwe, the Potawatomi, and the Ottawa peoples are still around today.*

As good historians, we will read and organize the information we learn in ways that make it easier to understand, and, in some cases, we will compare pieces of information. Good historians are intentional in how they seek out information specific to a question or area of interest. When historians read a lot of information, they try to focus in on the most relevant parts and organize them in a way that makes sense and will make it easier to compare information and answer their questions.

Remember our inquiry question is, "In the past, what was life like for the Indigenous people of Michigan?" What might we look for in the text to help us find the most relevant parts to read? We might look for the names like Potawatami, Ojibwe, or Ottawa because those are the Indigenous groups we have been discussing. Also, we want to know about "ways of life," so what else might we look for in the text? Pictures of houses or food. Let's take a look at these pages from our textbook, together. What do you notice about these two pages? What are they about? Do they help us understand our question? If you don't find the information in your textbook, I would like to you to scan the article from the Michigan Historical Society.

Next, students move into small groups and are given a graphic organizer with guiding questions (Figure 2.4). The graphic organizer also has one question highlighted, such that at least one student has been assigned each question for each of the three Indigenous groups.

Our inquiry question is broad. Sometimes, when we have a broad question, it's easier to locate good information to answer it if we break it down into smaller questions. In a minute, I'm going to give each of you a graphic organizer that looks like this. [Show students the graphic organizer.] *On your organizer, one group name—Potawatami, Ottawa, or Ojibwe—will be written at the top. Down below, just one of these specific questions about their way of life will be highlighted.* [Indicate and read the questions in Figure 2.4.] *Before you start reading, think about what you might look for in the text to get you to the right place to find the information to answer the question.*

Name:	
Group:	
Where did they live?	
What were their houses like?	
What did they eat?	
What was special about them?	
What did they make?	

Figure 2.4. Graphic Organizer Exploring Michigan's Indigenous People (adapted from the Michigan Citizenship Collaborative Curriculum [MC3], 2010). ©Michigan Citizenship Collaborative, 2010.

Each student scans the text with attention to their highlighted question, stopping to take notes when they locate the appropriate information. Once students have had the opportunity to answer their individual question, students gather in groups, each comprised of students who had different questions about the same Indigenous group. They then share the information they learned in order to answer their questions. While one student speaks, the other students in the group take notes on their own graphic organizers until all questions have been answered.

As a whole group, students share the information they found while the teacher records information on three large graphic organizers, identical to those used by the students. The graphic organizers can then be layered to form a table (Figure 2.5). After briefly demonstrating how to use the column and row headings to answer questions for each group (e.g., what were the Potowatmi homes like?), ask the students to make inferences about the similarities and differences in the daily lives of Indigenous people in the past.

Figure 2.5. Combined Graphic Organizers (Brugar & Roberts, 2015, p. 39).

3. Provide Closure

To conclude the lesson, remind students that good historians are critical readers, who use a variety of sources to answer their questions. As historians and students who gather information from a variety of sources, it is helpful to preview texts by scanning for clues to locate useful information. In other words, students scan to identify information that helps them answer their inquiry question. Being able to scan allows readers to review a greater number of sources to confirm what they know, note alternative responses, and create and demonstrate knowledge about a topic.

Individually, in small groups, and as a whole group, we worked to learn a little bit about the how the Potowatomi, the Ottawa, and the Ojibwe lived in the past. In order to learn about these groups of people, you used our guiding questions. [Refer to column one questions on the left side of the anchor chart.] *You also scanned the text for information to help answer those questions—you thought carefully about your questions and then searched the text, specifically looking for key words to help you locate the answers.*

Resources for Reading: 3-5

Student Resources for Reading (State-Specific Sample Resources):

Michigan History for Kids (Historical Society of Michigan, n.d.): This website includes historical information about Michigan; similar websites are available for most other states, often published by state historical societies or museums. https://hsmichigan.org/michigan-history-kids

State Historical Society Websites: Across the United States, state historical museums or historical societies are a wealth of archival and curated materials for teachers and students.

> **Student Resources for Reading (General Historical Resources):**
>
> *National Geographic Kids, U.S. States and Territories*: This website includes photos, facts, and history for individual states. https://kids.nationalgeographic.com/geography/states
>
> *A True Book: My United States Series* (various authors and years): This book series, published by Children's Press, includes informational books about each state, Puerto Rico, and Washington, DC.
>
> **Teacher Resources for Reading (Specific to Native Americans):**
>
> *Native Knowledge 360* (Smithsonian, 2024): This website is hosted by the Museum of the American Indian and includes instructional resources for teaching about Native Americans. https://americanindian.si.edu/nk360
>
> **Teacher Resources for Reading (General):**
>
> *Classroom Materials at the Library of Congress:* The Library of Congress offers a wide variety of primary source sets that you can search by keyword or browse by topic, era, or recommended grade level. https://www.loc.gov/classroom-materials/
>
> *Library of Congress: Finding Primary Sources*: Beyond the primary sources offered by the Library of Congress itself, the Library of Congress provides a full guide for finding additional primary sources in the form of curated sets, online collections, and connections with experts. https://www.loc.gov/programs/teachers/getting-started-with-primary-sources/finding/

Wrapping Up

Reading—the act of constructing and extracting meaning from a wide range of texts—is a social justice issue. So much of what we learn in school comes from the careful, critical, and targeted reading of text. In social studies learning and application, reading is essential to gathering information, discerning what is and isn't relevant to the question at hand, forming the basis of our belief systems, and taking informed action as citizens.

Investigating questions—our own and those posed by others—is at the heart of inquiry, in and outside of school. Preparing students with concrete strategies and tools to develop and confirm responses while reading reputable sources, is central to social studies inquiry and citizenry. This is why social studies matters in the real world and how active citizenship translates to people bringing different information and ideas to a community issue and working toward consensus or solutions.

Reading in social studies is essential to gathering information, which includes discerning what is and isn't needed to answer compelling and supporting questions about time periods, places, or ideas. Investigating such questions is at the heart of inquiry, sets the purpose for reading, and supports engagement with texts.

Chat and Change

"Chat and change" topics can be used as a menu of discussion starters for professional learning communities (PLCs), teacher education courses, or book clubs. You can also use them to guide your individual thinking about how to move the instructional practices in the chapter into your classroom.

- What are some specific skills associated with reading in the social studies? How might teachers of elementary-aged students build on skills introduced in previous grades?
- Do your students have an explicit purpose when they read in the social studies? If so, how is that purpose determined?
- Do your students know how to use their purposes for reading to guide their strategies for reading? How might you help them align purposes and strategies?
- In what ways are your students able to select their own topics and texts, based on their interests? How can you provide access to texts for students who are not yet reading fully independently?

References

Abdelrahman, M. S. H. B., & Bsharah, M. S. (2014). The effect of speed reading strategies on developing reading comprehension among the 2nd secondary students in English language. *English Language Teaching, 7*(6), 168–174.

Afflerbach, P., Pearson, P. D., & Paris, S. G. (2008). Clarifying differences between reading skills and reading strategies. *The Reading Teacher, 61*(5), 364–373.

Berkely, S., Scruggs, T. E., & Mastropieri, M. A. (2010). Reading comprehension instruction for students with learning disabilities, 1995–2006: A meta-analysis. *Remedial and Special Education, 31*(6), 423–436.

Brugar, K., & Roberts, K. L. (2015). Let's table it: Using tables to reflect on informational reading. *Oregon Journal for the Social Studies, 3*(2), 31–43.

Cabell, S. Q., & Hwang, H. (2020). Building content knowledge to boost comprehension in the primary grades. *Reading Research Quarterly, 55*(S), 99–107.

Cervetti, G. N., Pearson, P. D., Palincsar, A. S., Afflerbach, P., Kendeou, P., Biancarosa, G., Higgs, J., Fitzgerald, M. S., & Berman, A. I. (2020). How the Reading for Understanding initiative's research complicates the simple view of reading invoked in the science of reading. *Reading Research Quarterly, 55*(1), 161–172.

Coiro, J., & Dobler, E. (2007). Exploring the online reading comprehension strategies used by sixth-grade skilled readers to search for and locate information on the Internet. *Reading Research Quarterly, 42*(2), 214–257.

Cutting, L. E., Bailey, S. K., Barquero, L. A., & Aboud, K. (2015). Neurobiological bases of word recognition and reading comprehension. In C. M. Connor & P. McCardle (Eds.), *Advances in reading intervention: Research to practice to research* (pp. 73–84). Paul H. Brookes.

Duke, N. K., & Cartwright, K. B. (2021). The science of reading progresses: Communicating advances beyond the simple view of reading. *Reading Research Quarterly, 56*(51), S25–S44.

Joseph, L. M., Alber-Morgan, S., Cullen, J., & Rouse, C. (2016). The effects of self-questioning on reading comprehension: A literature review. *Reading & Writing Quarterly, 32*, 152–173.

Murphy, P. K., Wilkinson, I. A. G., Soter, A. O., Hennessey, M. N., & Alexander, J. F. (2009). Examining the effects of classroom discussion on students' high-level comprehension of text: A meta-analysis. *Journal of Educational Psychology, 101*(3), 740–764.

National Council for the Social Studies. (2013). *The college, career, and civic life (C3) framework for social studies state standards: Guidance for enhancing the rigor of K–12 civics, economics, geography, and history.* Authors.

National Governors Association Center for Best Practices, & Council of Chief State School Officers. (2010). *Common Core State Standards.* Authors.

Okkinga, M., van Steensel, R., van Gelderen, A. J. S., van Schooten, E., Sleegers, P. J. C., & Arends, L. R. (2018). Effectiveness of reading-strategy interventions in whole classrooms: A meta-analysis. *Educational Psychology Review, 30*, 1215–1239.

Pressley, M., & Afflerbach, P. (1995). *Verbal protocols of reading: The nature of constructively responsive reading.* Lawrence Erlbaum Associates.

Raphael, T. E. (1984). Teaching learners about sources of information for answering comprehension questions. *Journal of Reading Behavior, 27*, 303–311.

Raphael, T. E., & Au, K. H. (2005). QAR: Enhancing comprehension and test taking across grades and content areas. *The Reading Teacher, 59*, 206–221.

Scarborough, H. S. (2001). Connecting early language and literacy to later reading (dis)abilities: Evidence, theory, and practice. In S. B. Neuman & D. K. Dickinson (Eds.), *Handbook of early literacy research* (vol. 1, pp. 97–110). Guilford.

Shanahan, T., Collison, K., Carriere, C., Duke, N. K., Pearson, P. D., Schatschenider, C., & Toregesen, J. (2010). *Improving reading comprehension in kindergarten through 3rd grade: A practice guide (NCEE 2010-4038).* National Center for Education Evaluation and Regional Assistance, Institute of Education Sciences, U.S. Department of Education.

Taboada, A., & Guthrie, J. T. (2006). Contributions of student questioning and prior knowledge to construction of knowledge from reading information text. *Journal of Literacy Research, 38*(1), 1–35.

Wright, T. S. (2018–2019). Reading to learn from the start: The power of interactive read alouds. *American Educator, 42,* 4–8.

Children's Literature and Lesson Resources Referenced

Historical Society of Michigan. (n.d.). *Michigan history for kids.* Michigan Historical Society. https://hsmichigan.org/michigan-history-kids

Kalman, B. (2014). *Communication then and now.* Crabtree Classics.

Kalman, B. (2014). *Community helpers then and now.* Crabtree Classics.

Kalman, B. (2014). *Food and farming then and now.* Crabtree Classics.

Kalman, B. (2014). *School days.* Crabtree Classics.

Kalman, B. (2014). *Toys and games.* Crabtree Classics.

Kalman, B. (2014). *Travel.* Crabtree Classics.

Lassieur, A. (2011). *Cars 100 years ago.* Amicus.

Lassieur, A. (2011). *Clothes 100 years ago.* Amicus.

Lassieur, A. (2011). *Food 100 years ago.* Amicus.

Lassieur, A. (2011). *Phones 100 years ago.* Amicus.

Lassieur, A. (2011). *School 100 years ago*. Amicus.

Levine, E. (1992). *If you traveled west in a covered wagon*. Scholastic.

Library of Congress. (n.d.). *Primary source set: Child labor*. https://www.loc.gov/classroom-materials/child-labor/

Library of Congress. (n.d.). *Primary source set: Children's lives at the turn of the twentieth century*. https://www.loc.gov/classroom-materials/childrens-lives-at-the-turn-of-the-twentieth-century/

National Geographic Society. (2024). *U.S. states and territories*. National Geographic for Kids. https://kids.nationalgeographic.com/geography/states

National Museum of the American Indian. (2024). *Native knowledge 360*. National Museum of the American Indian, Smithsonian. https://americanindian.si.edu/nk360

Nelson, R. (2003, 2018). *Communication then and now*. LearnerClassroom.

Nelson, R. (2003, 2018). *Home then and now*. LearnerClassroom.

Nelson, R. (2003, 2018). *School then and now*. LearnerClassroom.

Nelson, R. (2003). *Toys and games then and now*. LearnerClassroom.

Nelson, R. (2003, 2018). *Transportation then and now*. LearnerClassroom.

Nelson, R. (2007). *Working then and now*. LearnerClassroom.

A True Book: My United States (series including books about each state, Puerto Rico, and Washington, DC). Children's Press.

CHAPTER 3

Writing
WRITING TO LEARN AND LEARNING TO WRITE

Just after lunch, first-grade students settle back into their classroom meeting area to continue their social studies unit on wants and needs. The students are preparing to coauthor a class book, explaining what wants and needs are and giving several examples of what the students want and need. Their teacher, Ms. V, is aware that this is a large and daunting task but is confident that working through the writing process as a whole class and with partners will support students in completing it.

As the class settles in, she begins, "In the last few days, we've been talking quite a bit about wants and needs. Think for just a minute on your own about what a want is." After a brief pause, she continues, "Now, turn to your elbow partner and share your thinking. What is a want?" As student discussion quiets down, she reiterates that "a want is something we would like to have. For example, I want a sparkle pen." She then asks them to consider what a need is and discuss with their elbow partners, followed by a reminder that "a need is something that is important and necessary for each of us—like food or water." She then directs students to discuss wants and needs with their elbow partners. After an interval this review, Ms. V prepares to model her own prewriting and tells the students, "When writers are preparing to write a book, just like we are, they don't just sit down and write the whole thing. That would be really hard and also probably not result in the best book. Writers use a process for writing that breaks it down into more manageable pieces and helps them to write the best book they can. Before they even put words on paper, writers start by thinking about what they want to write about and who they're writing for. This is part of 'prewriting,' which is thinking that comes before writing."

Ms. V continues, "Who do you think a good audience would be for our book about wants and needs?" After some discussion, the class decides that the book would be good for other first-grade classes learning about wants and needs. Mrs. V says, "OK, now that we know who we are writing for, we're ready to think about what information we're going to share. Each of us is going to think of several ideas of things we want and need, and then, tomorrow, we'll choose our favorites to write about."

Ms. V goes on to say, "One way to brainstorm ideas is to draw. I'm going to divide this paper in half, and, on this side, I'm going to write wants and draw things that I want. I'll label the other side needs and draw things I need." Ms. V spends a few minutes thinking of things she wants and needs, carefully considering whether each is a want or need and drawing a brief sketch of each on the correct side of the paper.

She says, "When I'm drawing, the idea is just to get the ideas down. It doesn't matter if the pictures are great because this is just where I'm keeping track of my ideas so I can remember them later. It is not my book page." After drawing three wants and three needs, Ms. V models labeling them, listening for sounds as she stretches each word.

The students then go off to create their own wants and needs prewriting illustrations. The steady hum of students sharing their ideas as they draw fills the room as Ms. V circulates, checking in to chat about ideas and assist with attempts to label the pictures.

The students in this vignette are, without a doubt, writers. While they didn't produce a piece of connected writing in this lesson, they did start the careful work of curating their ideas through prewriting. They're learning that writers are not gifted with the ability to sit down and create masterpieces in one go, but rather, they create good writing by putting work into the process of writing. They are learning that they, too, can be writers.

What Is Writing?

Writing and reading are reciprocal skills. We read texts to extract and construct meaning (RAND, 2002). (See Chapter 2.) We write to share what we know and are thinking—opinions, information and understandings, and real and imagined stories. Writing is also thinking because it requires us to consider ideas carefully enough to be able to share them in a way that others can understand, typically without our being there to clarify or answer questions. Writing is one way we send our thoughts out into the world to stand on their own.

Similar to reading, writing is also purpose-driven (e.g., Paré & Smart, 1994). How we write depends on what we are trying to accomplish and the audience. For example, if students are using writing to support a project advocating for composting in their school, they would need to approach the task differently for different audiences. A letter to the company that might do the composting, written to request information, would differ from a letter to district administrators, written to argue for the value of composting and to address concerns about required resources.

In its most simple form, writing is the process of putting words on paper to share ideas. At least for alphabetic languages, it involves taking ideas and representing them with abstract symbols that represent sounds. Those sounds combine to make words that carry meaning, which changes as words are combined in different ways. But writing is so much more than that and much, much more complex.

WHY IS WRITING IMPORTANT?

Writing is a powerful form of communication because it can be used to communicate with others across space and time. Sometimes, this is mundane—how often have you been grateful to your past self for leaving a note to remind your present self of an appointment or to remember your lunch? Other times, writing is a way to reach people we may never cross paths with, for example: this book! We would love to talk about all of the things in this book with each reader, but, since we probably can't, we wrote our ideas down and sent them out into the world on their own.

Writing makes our thinking visible to ourselves and others and allows us to share ideas. While not essential in all societies, in most modern societies, writing is a form of power because those who have writing skills can forward their ideas in ways that are not accessible to those who do not. Ideas that are written can be shared widely and quickly, and, if they are written well, can be quite persuasive.

In the social studies, writing and the writing process present opportunities for students to process and learn content (e.g., Graham et al., 2020) and to demonstrate a wide variety of what they know, think about, and consider. Writing in social studies is more than simply composing an answer to facilitate assessment of social studies knowledge. Writing provides students a space to formulate their ideas and frame their curiosities or to demonstrate a synthesis of information to share with a larger audience (De La Paz et al., 2016).

Pedagogies for Writing

Writing is often an iterative process. That is, our first attempt at writing something often isn't the final product, and getting to the final product is not a lockstep process. There are, of course, exceptions—it's much more likely that we take several passes at an annual holiday letter or class paper than a reminder to put the frozen pizza in the oven at 5:30 p.m. Part of learning to write effectively is learning to approach writing as a multistep, recursive process. However, effective writers also understand that not all writing purposes call for a polished product.

Too often, children are simply assigned writing and then expect that they can start at the top of the page and write a polished product in one go. That approach is pretty ineffective and generally results in writing that is . . . not great. The problem here is not that the students are poor writers, but rather, that they have not been taught a process for moving from ideas in their head to ideas written clearly enough to stand alone.

In this chapter, we're going to look closely at process writing. Process writing involves a recursive, five-part cycle: prewriting (sometimes called planning), drafting, editing, revising, and publishing. The writing process is a valuable tool because students who are taught a process approach to writing compose higher-quality texts than those who are not (e.g., Berninger et al., 2002; Graham et al., 2012; Graham & Sandmel, 2011).

> ## Writing Process
>
> **Prewriting:** Consider purpose, audience, message, form, and function; may include discussion, drawing, writing, or other modalities.
> **Drafting:** Write ideas in order or organize ideas; include main ideas and details.
> **Revising:** Review your draft and make improvements or changes to organization, ideas, word choice, level of detail, clarity.
> **Editing:** Review and make improvements to structural elements, such as spelling, punctuation, grammar, and capitalization.
> **Publishing:** Prepare your writing for sharing with others by creating a "clean" copy.

The writing process is recursive because writers don't always move through the steps one at a time, in order. For example, sometimes a writer might get as far as revising, then go back to prewriting to further develop a new idea that came about as part of a revision. Other times, writers may not complete the cycle; a draft may be all that's needed. For a letter to a friend, writers may not need or want to revise, edit, and create a polished copy.

In this chapter, the primary pedagogical focus is teaching students about process writing, itself. Specifically, we zoom in on prewriting and drafting in the K–2 lesson and drafting in the 3–5 lesson. The highlighted instructional practices, interactive writing and use of graphic organizers, have been found to be effective on their own and as an instructional component of the writing process.

In the K–2 lesson, the focus is on interactive writing, or joint composition, of text. In interactive writing lessons, the teacher addresses students' "developmental strengths and needs through explicit teaching, modeling, and involving children in writing" (Michigan Association of Intermediate School Administrators General Education Leadership Network Early Task Force [MAISA-GELN], 2023, p. 6). The general idea behind interactive writing is that it allows children the opportunity to observe how a skilled writer approaches writing, apprentice with a skilled writer, and approach problems that might arise in their independent writing with a high level of support.

Interactive writing is a practice that is beneficial primarily for children in the lower elementary grades (MAISA-GELN, 2023). Young students who engage in interactive writing instruction tend to outperform students who do not in communication of ideas, organization, word choice, sentence fluency, spelling, mechanics, and handwriting (e.g., Roth & Guinee, 2011).

The 3–5 lesson focuses on teaching students to use graphic organizers. In this lesson, they are specifically using graphic organizers as tools to support written summarization. With the use of graphic organizers in social studies, students are able to organize, personalize, make meaning, and reference information easily (Crawford & Carnine, 2000; MacKinnon & Deppell, 2005).

CLASSROOM APPLICATIONS, K–2

Writing in lower elementary classrooms can be quite challenging because students are doing the work to develop their ideas while simultaneously learning the mechanics (e.g., spelling, spacing, punctuation) that make them understandable to others. The goals of writing with young students should be to improve the skills of the writer and communicate ideas, not to produce perfectly polished pieces.

There are opportunities to teach skills in every stage of the writing process, but we can't teach all skills at once, and we need to give children multiple exposures and time to practice and develop the skills before we can expect them to master them. In a drafting lesson, such as the one that follows, a teacher might choose to support students to use classroom resources to spell sight words correctly, listen for sounds in words and match them to letters, form letters correctly, use punctuation, or develop any other one or two skills that would build on their strengths or support their needs.

CONNECTIONS TO THE *C3 FRAMEWORK* AND *COMMON CORE STATE STANDARDS*

In social studies, students use writing for many purposes and across disciplines. The *C3 Framework* places particular emphasis on the use of writing to communicate conclusions of inquiries, large and small. The lesson profiled here draws on economic concepts of wants and needs, but the idea of supporting a claim with reasons applies to all disciplines.

Individually and with others, students . . .

> D4.1.K–2: Construct an argument with reasons (National Council for the Social Studies [NCSS], 2013, p. 60).

The *Common Core State Standards for English Language Arts* address writing in three primary genres: opinion, informational, and narrative (National Governors Association Center for Best Practices & Council of Chief State School Officers, 2010). The text students are writing in this lesson is mostly informational, though there is a bit of opinion in the mix when children explain why they want particular items. The lines are blurry, and that's OK! Students are also working to create a text together, which the standards refer to as a shared writing project.

W.K.2: Use a combination of drawing, dictating, and writing to compose informative/explanatory texts in which they name what they are writing about and supply some information about the topic.
W.1.2: Write informative/explanatory texts in which they name a topic, supply some facts about the topic, and provide some sense of closure.
W.2.2: Write informative/explanatory texts in which they introduce a topic, use facts and definitions to develop points, and provide a concluding statement or section.
W.K-2.7: Participate in shared research and writing projects (p. 19).

Writing in Action, K–2

This lesson builds on the opening vignette. When we last looked in on them, students had gone off to create their own pictorial lists of wants and needs. Their teacher was circulating, helping them consider whether items were best classified as wants or needs, and supporting them as they labeled each item. At the close of their writing time, students were guided through a lesson in which they carefully selected one item from each category that they wanted to include in the class book. In the lesson that follows, students complete (at least for now) the prewriting stage and begin moving into the drafting stage of their writing.

1. Introduce the Lesson

Gather students as a whole group to begin the writing session. Be sure to post the list you modeled creating in the previous lesson so that it is visible to all students. Students should have their own lists as well as a pencil (and clipboard, if they are not at tables or desks) with them.

We've been hard at work on our prewriting for our "Wants and Needs" book. We each brainstormed a lot of good ideas, and then narrowed them down to one favorite want and one favorite need. You can see my favorite ideas circled on my list. [Point to the list.] *Today, we're going to do two things. First, we're going to finish our prewriting. That means we're going to finish thinking about the ideas we want to share. Then, we're going to start on our drafts of our book pages. That means we're going to write our ideas down. We might still make some changes before our pages go into the book.*

2. Teach the Lesson Using a Research-Based Instructional Practice (here, process writing [e.g., Berninger et al., 2002; Graham & Sandmel, 2011] and interactive writing [e.g., Roth & Guinee, 2011])

OK. Let's finish our prewriting. Now that we know what items from our list we want to write about, we have to think about what we want to say. Remember that our audience is students in other classes that are learning about wants and needs. Our book will be pretty boring and other kids might not learn much about wants and needs if we just tell them what each of us wants and what each of us needs. What else could we tell them that would help them understand?

Facilitate a class discussion about the kinds of information students might share. Most likely, they will decide that, at a minimum, other kids would need to know why they want and need things, but they may have other ideas, too.

I'm going to take just a minute to look at the two items I circled and think about why I want ice cream and why I need shoes. You can look at your items and think about why you want one and need the other. [Pause briefly, and model thinking. Then, model explaining.] *OK. I'm ready and I have some ideas. I might not write all of them, but I'm going to tell you about all of them.*

For my want, I chose ice cream. I want ice cream because I really like sweet foods. Also, ice cream is cold, and so it's extra good on a hot day. For my need, I chose to write about shoes. I need shoes because they keep my feet warm. I also need shoes so that I don't injure my feet when I'm walking outside or someplace very hot or very cold. Now it's your turn to share. Everyone put your finger on the item you chose for what you want. Now, turn to your elbow partner. Start by telling them what you want, then tell them why you want it. Be sure that each of you gets a turn. [Circulate and scaffold this process as needed. When everyone has had a chance to share what they want and why with a partner, invite a few students to share with the class. Prompt as needed for detail. Next, repeat the process with needs.]

You all have such good ideas! I can tell you've really thought carefully about this. Yesterday, we used drawing and labeling to help us think through our prewriting. Just now, we used talking to think through our prewriting. Now we're going to start drafting our pages. When we draft, we write the words that we think we want to put in our book. We're going to do some work to get our writing just the way we want it later, but, for now, we're going to concentrate on writing a clear sentence or two to share what we want and why.

[Display a new piece of chart paper.] *OK. I'm going to practice saying the first part of my "want" message a couple times. My first sentence is going to tell my reader what I want. I want ice cream. I want ice cream. Now, I'm going to count those words on my fingers while I say them. I want ice cream. Four! I'm going to draw four lines to help me remember to write each word in my sentence.* [Draw four lines on the paper. Count them, then point to each line as you say one word of your sentence.] *What's my first word?* [Students will most likely respond "I," but you can repeat the sentence again as you point if they do not.] *Yes, "I." I'm going to write that on the first line.*

Model reading the sentence from the beginning while pointing to the lines to determine the second word. Model stretching any words that the class wouldn't know how to spell and using your list to copy the spelling of your chosen item (even if the spelling is not conventional). Read the full sentence aloud when you are finished.

Repeat this process with a second sentence describing why you want the item. As you write the second sentence, invite children to "share the pen" for some words. Depending on students' strengths and needs, you might call on them to use classroom resources to write known words, such as "want" or "good." Alternatively, if you want to focus on stretching words or letter formation, you may have children write some or all of the letters in words that they need to stretch to spell. It is generally not a good idea to have the children write every word as it will make the process very slow and water down the focus on your instructional points.

For younger children and emergent writers, you can modify the writing to be shorter (e.g., one sentence: "I want ice cream because it tastes good"). You can also provide additional support by sitting with a small group of children who might need the most support as they write their own sentences. For older children and more experienced writers, you can model more detailed writing, perhaps adding two separate sentences of explanation. In all cases, children should be encouraged to support each other by doing things such as sharing their ideas, reading their sentences aloud to each other, and helping each other stretch words.

Depending on the time available, children's stamina for writing, and the level of support needed, you may write about both wants and needs in the same lesson or write about them on separate days. If you do them on the same day, you only need to model once—having children watch you write about both will tax their attention spans and probably not provide much more benefit. If children are going to write about wants and needs on separate days, you'll either want to model again or remind them of the process.

3. Provide Closure

Today we finished up our prewriting process. Remember that yesterday we did some drawing of wants and needs to create lists of ideas, we labeled the items, and we circled the wants and needs we wanted to write about. Today, we finished prewriting by thinking and talking about why we wanted or needed these things. Prewriting helps us get our ideas ready so that, when we write, we can focus mostly on getting our ideas into words on the paper without having to come up with the ideas at the same time.

Next, we started our drafts. After we practiced what we wanted to say in our first sentence a few times, we counted the words and made one line for each word. Then, we wrote the words, one at a time, rereading our sentence each time we wrote a word to make sure we didn't get mixed up or lose our place.

When we take our time to use the writing process, writing feels a bit easier, and it can help make our writing more interesting and informative for our audience. So far, we have done prewriting and drafting for our book pages. Tomorrow, we'll read what we have so far and learn about revising our work to make our ideas as clear and interesting as possible.

Resources for Writing: K-2

Student Resources for Wants and Needs:

Wants and Needs Collection (Korenek, Epic Books): This collection of nine books on the topics of wants and needs and other economic concepts includes four books with the "read to me" feature. https://www.getepic.com/collection/338874/wants-and-needs

Those Shoes (Boelts, 2009): This book shares the story of a young boy who wants a new pair of fancy shoes, but his grandmother says they only have room for wants, not needs.

Teacher Resources for Creating

K–3 Essential 6, Bullet 1: Interactive writing experience sample video (Michigan Virtual, n.d.): This video shows a small-group interactive writing lesson. (Note that, while this and the following resource were produced in Michigan, they are based on a comprehensive review of nationwide research.) https://www.youtube.com/watch?v=YS9lp_G0U50&t=14s

Essential Instructional Practices in Early Literacy: K–3, Essential 6 (Michigan Virtual, n.d.): This self-paced instructional module provides additional information on research-based writing practices. https://literacyessentials.org/literacy-essentials/professional-learning/k-3-modules/

Extending Interactive Writing into Grades 2–5 (Roth & Dabrowski, 2014): This open-access article describes interactive writing pedagogy for more developed writers.

The Writing Strategies Book: Your Everything Guide to Developing Skilled Writers (Serravallo, 2017): This book includes three hundred research-aligned strategies for teaching writing at various grade levels and at each stage of the writing process.

CLASSROOM APPLICATIONS, 3–5

All learners can engage in each step of the writing process with appropriate scaffolds and supports. However, the experiences of students in upper elementary grades with prewriting and drafting look a bit different, depending on their previous experiences and writing abilities. In social studies, prewriting is an opportunity for students to consider the inquiry question or prompt being presented. Then, writers use that prewriting experience to draft or share preliminary thoughts and ideas in writing. In this lesson, students will use prewriting as a scaffolded approach to drafting.

CONNECTIONS TO THE *C3 FRAMEWORK* AND *COMMON CORE STATE STANDARDS*

In social studies, writing is a means of communicating ideas and understandings as students engage in the inquiry process outlined in the *C3 Framework*. In this lesson, students consider what they know and understand about geographic regions of the United States in order to make a claim and support their claim with evidence. Primarily, this lesson addresses *C3* indicators related to constructing arguments and explanations supported by evidence.

D4.1.3–5. Construct arguments using claims and evidence from multiple sources.
D4.2.3–5. Construct explanations using reasoning, correct sequence, examples, and details with relevant information and data (NCSS, 2013, p. 60).

As mentioned for the K–2 lesson, the *Common Core State Standards for English Arts* address writing in three primary genres: opinion, informational, and narrative. For this lesson, students are providing an opinion in response to the prompt, "Which region of the United States would you most like to visit?" However, they are also supporting that opinion with factual information. As a result, the genre is a bit of hybrid between opinion and informational writing and addresses standards in both areas.

W.3.1.a: Introduce the topic or text they are writing about, state an opinion, and create an organizational structure that lists reasons.
W.3.1.b: Provide reasons that support the opinion.
W3.1.d: Provide a concluding statement or section.
W.4.1.a: Introduce a topic or text clearly, state an opinion, and create an organizational structure in which related ideas are grouped to support the writer's purpose.
W.4.1.b: Provide reasons that are supported by facts and details.
W.4.1.d: Provide a concluding statement or section related to the opinion presented.
W.5.1.a: Introduce a topic or text clearly, state an opinion, and create an organizational structure in which ideas are logically grouped to support the writer's purpose.
W.5.1.b: Provide reasons that are supported by facts and details.
W.5.1.c: Link opinion and reasons using words, phrases, and clauses (e.g., *consequently, specifically*).

W.5.1.d: Provide a concluding statement or section related to the opinion presented (National Governors Association Center for Best Practices & Council of Chief State School Officers, 2010, p. 20).

Writing in Action, 3–5

This lesson builds on students' prior learning about the geographic regions of the United States and the ways in which students use writing to summarize and synthesize their learning. In the lesson, students first use a graphic organizer to think through, organize, and record their learning. The completion of this graphic organizer is an example of prewriting and tracking their thinking in a linear way. Then, they use that graphic organizer as source material as they reorganize their thinking into a paragraph for an outside audience.

1. Introduce the Lesson

Prior to this lesson, students will have engaged in a discussion-based prewriting activity associated with the geographic regions of North America (i.e., the Midwest, the Northeast, the Southeast, the Southwest, the West). In their discussion, students identified various attributes or characteristics of each region.

Yesterday, we discussed the different geographic regions of North America and some of the things that make each region unique. I recorded some of your discussion points on the board so we might reference these prewriting notes as each of you begins to draft about one region in particular.

Remember, as writers we follow a process—we don't simply sit down and write all the ideas in our head as they come to us. Yesterday, as a group we discussed the regions of North America as a prewriting activity. Today, we are going to work individually to draft a response to a prompt about one of them.

2. Teach the Lesson Using a Research-Based Instructional Practice (Use of Graphic Organizers [e.g., Gould, 2010; Monte-Sano et al., 2014])

The prompt I would like you to be thinking about is, "Which geographic region of the United States would you most like to visit and why?" Yesterday, we talked about a lot of possible answers to this question. Today, we're going to organize our ideas—still part of prewriting—and then draft an answer. To get started organizing our ideas, I would like you to take the piece of paper at your desk and fold it in half and then in half again (hot dog and then hamburger).

Now your paper has four squares. Please label the squares "1," "2," "3," and "4." The numbers should be small so we have most of the square for our ideas. Let's add more one thing, a circle in the center. [See Figure 3.1.] Remember our prompt: "Which geographic region of the United States would you most like to visit and why?" Your response to which geographic region you would most like to visit will go in this center circle. Think for a moment, and then, in that circle, write the region you would most like to visit.

WRITING   41

Figure 3.1. Blank Student Organizer, Credit: Jude Roberts.

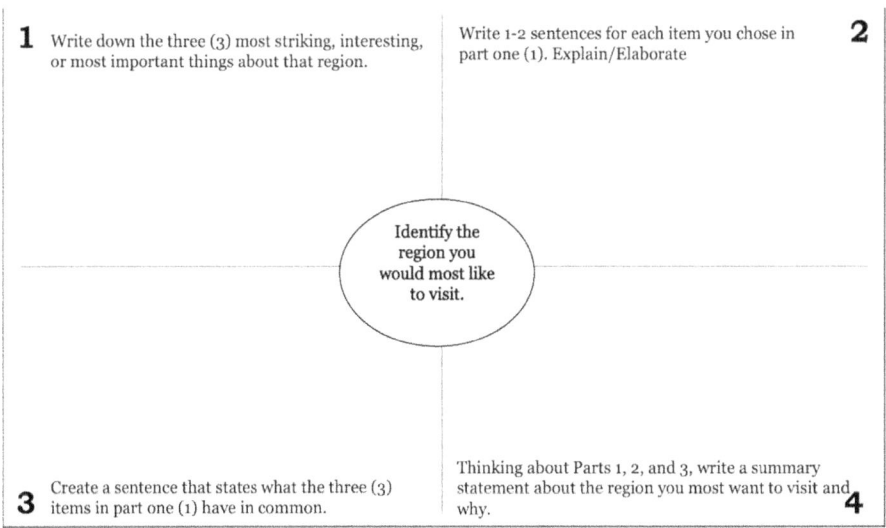

Figure 3.2. Four-Square Organizer with Prompts.

We have each identified the region we would most like to visit. [You may choose to ask students to identify the region they have selected by a simple raising of hands before moving on.] *Now, we can now approach the second part of the prompt, "why." In the square you have labeled "1," I would like you to write down the three most striking, interesting, or important things about that region.* [See Figure 3.2 for a version of the organizer with prompts and Appendix A for a generic version. Provide students time to write.]

42   CHAPTER 3

When we engage in prewriting, or other stages of the writing process, not everything students write in their notes will be used for the next stage of writing. This is the case with square 1 of the graphic organizer. Square 1 of the organizer creates space for students to reflect on the topic and frame their thinking. In squares 2 through 4, students have opportunities to demonstrate expanding those ideas, adding additional detail and context, and summarizing their ideas.

Let's move on to square 2. In this square, I would like you to elaborate on those three things you noted in square 1 and write one or two sentences for each item you chose in square 1. Who can tell me what "elaborate" means or provide another word that means the same thing? [Allow students time to respond before clarifying.] *Yes, elaborate means give more details. We've already done some of this thinking. This is a great opportunity to use some of the prewriting notes we have on the board!* [Provide students time to write, supporting students in using the notes on the board, as needed. They may also come up with additional ideas.]

Next, we are going to move to square 3. Here we will create a sentence that states what the three things in square 1 have in common. [Provide students time to write.]

Last, in square 4 we will write a summary statement about the region and the three items you chose to put in square 1. Your summary statement should clearly share which region you want to visit and why. [Provide students time to write. See Figure 3.3 for an example of a completed student organizer.]

To complete the graphic organizer, students are asked to unpack their thinking with each square demonstrating a more sophisticated way of thinking (following a progression through Anderson and colleagues' [2001] revised version of Bloom's taxonomy). In the final stage of the lesson, writers use the graphic organizer as a source

Figure 3.3.   Completed Student Organize, Credit; Jude Roberts.

of material to compose a paragraph. Square 4 of the organizer becomes their opening thesis statement or claim. Students will use their ideas and supporting details from square 2 to support their claim. Lastly, their square 3 sentence serves as a conclusion. *Do you know what we just did? We drafted some great text that we can rearrange to write a full paragraph! Sometimes, the way we think about what we want to say is different from what our final product looks like. When we put information into our graphic organizer, we went in order from square 1 to square 4. Each time we moved to a new square, we used our thinking in the previous boxes to help us decide what to write.*

When we draft our paragraph using this information, we're going to use a different order because, now, we aren't moving through our own thought process; we're thinking about how to share our most important ideas with others. Square 1 of the graphic organizer contains just enough information to get us thinking, but isn't really enough for readers to understand why we think the region is worth visiting. Instead, we're going to open our paragraph with our big idea.

It took us a lot of thinking to get to our biggest idea, which is our claim. So, in the graphic organizer, it's in square 4. Square 4 will be your first sentence, or your claim. Then, you will use the great details you came up with in square 2 as evidence to support your claim. Those are the next sentences in your paragraph. Finally, you will wrap up your paragraph by reminding readers of your big idea. You can do that by using the statement in square 3.

3. Provide Closure

Today we learned that you can organize your ideas on a graphic organizer and reorganize those ideas into a paragraph. Remember, as writers, you are engaged in a writing process including prewriting and drafting, which we did today. And tomorrow we will edit and revise.

Read your paragraph aloud to your elbow partner. It probably sounds pretty good, but you might notice a place or two where you might improve. [Provide time.] *Tomorrow, we will revise and peer edit.*

Resources for Writing: 3-5

Student Resources for US Regions:

Kids Discover, Regions of North America (Kids Discover, n.d.): This hard copy or e-copy magazine presents students with an overview of the regions of the United States and specific information about each region with text and images. https://online.kidsdiscover.com/unit/regions-of-north-america?gad_source=1&gclid=CjwKCAjwuMC2BhA7EiwAmJKRrJLNwPr0zvLum_-hLxTZUuZOgpoqKd_pvyAs-zxOyoy9A3nlMSMCkxoCfxsQAvD_BwE

U.S. States and Territories (National Geographic Kids, 2024): This kid-friendly website allows students to explore geographic information about each of the United States. https://kids.nationalgeographic.com/geography/states

> *A True Book: The U.S. Regions* (Rau, Children's Press, 2012): This series of informational texts describes the regions of the United States geographically, economically, and historically.
>
> **Teacher Resources for Writing:**
>
> *Essential Practices in Literacy: Grades 4–5* (MAISA-GELN, 2016): This is a collection of ten research-based literacy practices for classrooms; *Essential* 6 is focused on writing. https://literacyessentials.org/downloads/gelndocs/essential_instructionalliteracygr4-5.pdf
>
> *National Geographic Regions* (National Geographic, 2024): This website includes maps and articles about the United States and its regions. The articles span a broad range of topics for teachers to explore and use to connect with students. https://education.nationalgeographic.org/resource/united-states-regions/
>
> *The Writing Strategies Book: Your Everything Guide to Developing Skilled Writers* (Serravallo, 2017): This book includes three hundred research-aligned strategies for teaching writing at various grade levels and at each stage of the writing process.

Wrapping Up

Writing is important for both building understanding of and communicating ideas in all disciplines of social studies. However, it can be challenging for students to convert the ideas in their heads into written text that can be understood by a specific audience. It is necessary to socialize students to understand writing as a process that results in a product. Teaching students a process approach for writing helps them move from their own thinking to recording ideas in a form that can be shared with others beyond the immediate space and time—a crucial skill in civics, economics, history, and geography.

Chat and Change

"Chat and change" topics can be used as a menu of discussion starters for Professional Learning Communities (PLCs), teacher education courses, or book clubs. You can also use them to guide your individual thinking about how to move the instructional practices in the chapter into your classroom.

- Share examples of the kinds of writing your students do as part of social studies.
- Considering your state social studies and English language arts standards, what are appropriate writing skills to support social studies instruction in your classroom?
- Considering your state social studies and English language arts standards, what are your students' strengths and needs related to writing? What is your evidence?
- How do you guide your students to break writing tasks down into manageable pieces?
- What issues do your students run into when writing independently? How can you teach about and model strategies to address those issues?

References

Anderson, L. W., & Krathwohl, D. R. (Eds.). (2001). *A taxonomy for learning, teaching, and assessing: A revision of Bloom's Taxonomy of educational objectives* (complete edition). Longman.

Berninger, V. W., Vaughan, K., Abbott, R. D., Begay, K., Coleman, K. B., Curtain, G., Hawkins, J. M., & Graham, S. (2002). Teaching spelling and composition alone and together: Implications for the simple view of writing. *Journal of Educational Psychology*, 94, 291–304.

Crawford, D. B., & Carnine, D. (2000). Comparing the effects of textbooks in eighth-grade U.S. history: Does conceptual organization help? *Education and Treatment of Children*, 4(23), 387–422.

De La Paz, S., Monte-Sano, C., Felton, M., Croninger, R., Jackson, C., & Piantedosi, K. W. (2016). A historical writing apprenticeship for adolescents: Integrating disciplinary learning with cognitive strategies. *Reading Research Quarterly*, 52(1), 31–52.

Gould, J. (2010). *Four square for writing assessment*. Teaching and Learning Company.

Graham, S., Kiuhara, S. A., & McKay, M. (2020). The effects of writing on learning in science, social studies, and mathematics: A meta-analysis. *Review of Educational Research*, 90(2), 189–226.

Graham, S., McKeown, D., Kiuhara, S., & Harris, K. R. (2012). A meta-analysis of writing instruction for students in the elementary grades. *Journal of Educational Psychology*, 104(4), 879–896.

Graham, S., & Sandmel, K. (2011). The process writing approach: A meta-analysis. *Journal of Educational Research*, 104, 396–407.

MacKinnon, G. R., & Deppell, M. (2005). Concept mapping: A unique means for negotiating meaning in professional studies. *Journal of Educational Multimedia and Hypermedia*, 3(14), 291–315.

Michigan Virtual. (n.d.). *K–3 essential 6, bullet 1: Interactive writing experience sample video* [Video]. YouTube. https://www.youtube.com/watch?v=YS9lp_G0U50&t=14s

Michigan Virtual. (n.d.). *Essential instructional practices in early literacy: K–3 essential 6* [Online Module]. https://literacyessentials.org/literacy-essentials/professional-learning/k-3-modules/

Michigan Association of Intermediate School Administrators General Education Leadership Network Early Literacy Task Force. (2016). *Essential instructional practices in literacy. Grades 4 to 5*. Authors.

Michigan Association of Intermediate School Administrators General Education Leadership Network Early Literacy Task Force. (2023). *Essential instructional practices in early literacy: K to 3*. Authors.

Monte-Sano, C., De La Paz, S., & Felton, M. (2014). *Reading, thinking, and writing about history: Teaching argument writing to diverse learners in the common core classroom, grades 6–12*. Teachers College Press.

National Council for the Social Studies. (2013). *The college, career, and civic life (C3) framework for social studies state standards: Guidance for enhancing the rigor of k–12 civics, economics, geography, and history*. Authors.

National Governors Association Center for Best Practices & Council of Chief State School Officers. (2010). *Common Core State Standards*. Authors.

Paré, A., & Smart, G. (1994). Observing genres in action: Towards a research methodology. In A. Freedman & P. Medway (Eds.), *Genre and the New Rhetoric*. Taylor and Francis.

RAND Reading Study Group. (2002). *Reading for understanding: Toward an R & D program in reading comprehension*. RAND.

Roth, K., & Dabrowski, J. (2014). Extending interactive writing into grades 2–5. *Reading Teacher, 68*(1), 33–44.

Roth, K., & Guinee, K. (2011). Ten minutes a day: The impact of interactive writing instruction on first graders' independent writing. *Journal of Early Childhood Literacy, 11*(3), 331–361.

Serravallo, J. (2017). *The writing strategies book: Your everything guide to developing skilled writers.* Heinemann.

Children's Literature and Lesson Resources Referenced

Boelts, M. (2009). *Those shoes.* Candlewick. Korenek, S. (curator). (n.d.). *Wants and needs.* Get Epic! https://www.getepic.com/collection/338874/wants-and-needs

National Geographic Society. (2024). *U.S. states and territories.* National Geographic for Kids. https://kids.nationalgeographic.com/geography/states

Rau, D. M. (2012). *Northeast.* Children's Press.

Rau, D. M. (2012). *Midwest.* Children's Press.

Rau, D. M. (2012). *West.* Children's Press.

Rau, D. M. (2012). *Southwest.* Children's Press.

Rau, D. M. (2012). *Southeast.* Children's Press.

CHAPTER 4

Speaking
DEVELOPING ARGUMENT AND EXPLANATION

As third-grade students settle into a class meeting after lunch, Mr. B begins a discussion with a simple question: "Who are you?" Predictably, the students respond with their first or full names. Then, Mr. B asks again, "Who are you?" The children glance at one another and are a bit puzzled. A few children giggle. Mr. B repeats, "Who are you?" After a beat, he says, "We are more than simply our names. How many of you are a brother or sister?" Many students raise their hands. "How many of you play sports?" Almost all the children raise their hands.

Mr. B responds, "So, there are siblings, big brothers, and little sisters in our class. Some of those brothers and sisters are also athletes. How many of you have a pet?" A few hands rise, and the teacher calls on a child, "What pet do you have?" The child responds, "I have a cat and a turtle." "Wonderful! So, when I ask the question 'who are you?' you can tell me your name and tell me you are a cat and turtle owner."

After giving a few students the opportunity to introduce themselves in this way, Mr. B explains, "There are many ways we can answer that question and describe ourselves. If you asked me this question, I might say, 'I am a teacher. I am a swimmer. And I am the tallest person in the room today!'" The children giggle. "Now, I would like you to talk with a partner. Take turns asking each other, 'Who are you?' When your partner asks who you are, give them an answer that describes at least three different things about you."

After a few minutes, Mr. B asks one of the children to share her three descriptors and records them on the board. He says, "Thank you for sharing that you are a soccer player, older sister, and a reader. Is there someone who has one of these descriptions in common with our classmate?" Several hands go up, and the teacher calls on one student who also identifies as a soccer player. That student adds, "I am also an only child, and I am a swimmer."

Mr. B solicits several more examples, each time asking students to connect with one descriptor from the previous speaker to focus the children's attention on the importance of each speaker's contribution. Then, in an effort to summarize this conversation and highlight that the students have both similarities and differences, the teacher asks students, "What are some observations or things we notice about the ways we identified ourselves?"

Mr. B then pivots the conversation and asks the children to consider another question: "Where are you?" He prompts them to think about at least three ways to answer this ques-

tion. The children move into conversations, noting they are in the classroom, at school, and in their town and state. The children discuss where they are for several minutes before the teacher brings them together as a whole class and asks for a few volunteers to share their responses to this question. Then, the teacher shares his observations of their responses, those he heard in small conversations as well as the whole-group examples.

The challenge in many classrooms is creating the space for authentic speaking opportunities for students. In this chapter's vignette, students participated in an experience that provided authentic opportunities to verbalize what they know, noticed, wondered, and learned as a result of a common experience. The students (Brugar, 2023) identified places familiar to them. As social studies students, children often learn about people, places, and events that are far away. But, as elementary social studies teachers, we consistently relate those events, places, and people to the lives and experiences of students.

In this vignette, the students talked about a fairly low-stakes topic; something that involves little risk. In social studies instruction, some topics will be low stakes. However, there will also be times when students need to discuss high-stakes or controversial topics. Controversial topics are those that raise "legitimate, competing points of view about questions that matter to people" (Hess, 2004, as paraphrased in Rodriguez & Swalwell, 2022, p. 38). Establishing norms and expectations for such discussions is essential. Further, teaching students the skills to engage in discussions effectively builds the foundation for productive and civil discourse, even, and especially when students hold opposing views.

What Is Speaking?

Alongside writing and creating, speaking is a productive language skill that is used to share, clarify, and negotiate ideas. Like writing and creating, speaking can be done in collaboration with others to exchange or negotiate ideas. It can also be done alone as a way to work through thinking and clarify one's own thoughts or a rehearsal for writing, creating, or more formal speaking. Unlike writing, spoken or signed language comes naturally for nearly all typically developing children, given appropriate exposure (e.g., Feldman, 2019). (Note that "speaking" in this chapter refers to both spoken and signed language.)

Most students learn to speak for basic communicative purposes in daily life prior to entering your classroom. Speech is likely to develop naturally; however, nuanced ways of speaking can and often need to be taught and learned. Like skilled writers, skilled speakers attend to audience, purpose, word choice, tone, and rhetorical devices. Speaking also requires having interpersonal skills, such as listening carefully and evaluating the ideas of others, in order to respond in context-appropriate ways.

Speaking is a key component of effective collaboration with others. As a discipline, social studies is inherently collaborative. Students are called upon to use a variety of speaking skills to ask and answer questions, provide explanations, consider and respond to different points of view and alternative ways of thinking, share findings from research or inquiry, and engage in civic action; all of these endeavors typically require speaking with others.

WHY IS SPEAKING IMPORTANT?

In the social studies, generally, and in civic participation, specifically, students use speaking skills to contribute to consequential conversations and to advocate for their ideas. In civic education, students learn "to contribute appropriately to public processes and discussions of real issues. Their contributions to public discussions may take many forms, ranging from personal testimony to abstract arguments" (Swan et al., 2013, p. 31). Speaking transcends school purposes and moves into informed action in real-world contexts. Ultimately, most ideas are only as effective as people's ability to share them clearly.

Throughout this book, from chapter to chapter, we share reciprocal processes—reading and writing, listening and speaking, viewing and creating. These practices happen independently and can happen at different times. Speaking and listening are a bit different from the other two pairs. The time lapse between speaking and listening may be much shorter and, in some cases, nonexistent, making speaking and listening much more difficult to separate, instructionally, than the other two pairs. For this reason, in this chapter, our primary focus is on speaking with references to necessary listening to facilitate students' speaking skills.

Pedagogies for Speaking

As noted above, most typically developing children naturally acquire a level of speaking or signing that is adequate for everyday communicative needs. While speaking may seem like a fairly straightforward skill, learning to do so in particular ways that enhance learning in the social studies and the ability to participate fully in civic life typically requires instruction. All the research-based pedagogies described in this chapter are designed to provide overt structure to students as they learn to use speaking in these ways, allowing them to focus more of their attention on the content of their discussions as they learn to effectively share their ideas.

Speaking covers a wide array of skills. In this chapter, we are zooming in on foundational skills for engaged discussion because discussion is essential for both social construction of knowledge and broader civic participation and communication. While there are many research-based ways to support discussion, in this chapter we focus on the use of sentence frames, questioning, and models for structured discussion. Examples of each of these in action can be found in either the K–2 or 3–5 classroom applications; however, all can be modified to work for students across the K–5 grade span.

The first research-based pedagogy is the use of sentence frames to support students to start discussions and build on the ideas of others. Sentence frames are generic cloze sentences that help students structure how they share their ideas but leave the ideas themselves up to the students.

Sentence frames are particularly useful for students as they learn to express more controversial or increasingly complex ideas within the disciplines (e.g., Hoffman & Zollman, 2016). The use of sentence frames is appropriate for all learners as a support for building content-area vocabulary and knowledge through discussion (e.g., Bluffington et al., 2017) and is also highly recommended for multilingual learners (Baker et al., 2014).

The options for sentence frames are just about unlimited, but sticking to a small number, at least at first, helps students to use them as a tool and to internalize the language. For this reason, it's helpful to keep the frames generic enough to be used in discussions on lots of different topics. For example, the following text frames might be used to start a discussion or introduce a new idea:

- One thing that I thought was interesting was _____.
- I am wondering about _____.
- Something that didn't quite make sense to me was _____.

Alternatively, the following sentence frames can be used to support students as they build upon or work to understand the ideas of others:

- Can you say more about what you meant when you said _____?
- How do you think _____ fits with other things we have learned about _____?
- When you said _____ it reminded me of _____.

It is important to teach, post, and model use of the sentence frames during class and small-group discussions. From there, you can explicitly remind students to use them in their own small group and paired discussions. While circulating, provide reminders and praise students who are trying them out and making sure the frames are easily accessible in these spaces (e.g., included in group folders, on bookmarks, as a table resource). Teaching about and posting sentence frames is only valuable if students are then expected to use them and supported in using them in real discussions, consistently, until they no longer need the support (e.g., Hoffman & Zollman, 2016).

It is also important to keep in mind that sentence frames are a scaffold to support access to participation in discussions and are not meant to constrain students' options for participation or what they choose to share (e.g., Barko-Alva & Chang-Bacon, 2023). While sentence frames can be an important support as students learn to use language to discuss ideas in new ways, some students may not need the sentence frames or may not need them as long as other students to accomplish the same discussion goals. The ultimate goal is for students to internalize the processes for starting and continuing engaged discussions with peers and for the frames to gradually become less necessary.

A second research-based pedagogy is questioning. Here, questioning does not refer to teachers asking students questions but, rather, teachers teaching children speaking skills so that they can ask their own questions, either about sources or of each other. Questioning is a strategy that can be used even with the youngest of students (e.g., Gregory & Cahill, 2010) and that, when done with intention, can be used by students to frame inquiry and consider information from a variety of perspectives (Fisher & Frey, 2018). Asking questions during reading is also an important way in which readers monitor comprehension and serves as a support for independent learning (Joseph et al., 2016).

There are lots of different research-based pedagogies for questioning. Two commonly used in classrooms include the following:

- Question-Answer Relationships (QAR; Raphael, 1982, 1984): Students are taught to ask four types of questions, two for which answers can be found directly in the text and two for which answers require outside information. Answers to "right there" questions can be found in a single sentence in the source, while answers to "think and search" questions require gathering information from across the source. Responses to "author and you" questions require information from the source and background knowledge, while "on your own" questions require only prior knowledge. (For more on this strategy, see Chapter 2.)
- Questioning the Author (QtA; Beck et al., 1996, 2021): QtA is an excellent fit for social studies because it integrates questioning with perspective taking. Students are taught to think about the author's purpose for writing and perspective as well as about how other authors or they themselves may have different perspectives. The strategy suggests the use of generic questions to
  - initiate discussion (e.g., "What is the author trying to say?")
  - focus on the message (e.g., "The words say ____, but what does that really mean?")
  - link information (e.g., "What information did the author share that connects with _____?")
  - consider clarity (e.g., "Did the author explain that well? What's missing?")
  - reference the text (e.g., "Did the author say anything about _____?")

  This last category, in particular, also supports the social studies disciplinary skill of backing claims with evidence.

The classroom applications for this chapter integrate aspects of both sentence frames and questioning pedagogies. In addition to supporting effective speaking skills for discussion, combining these pedagogical supports has been shown to have strong effects on comprehension (Rosenshine et al., 1996).

Scaffolded approaches to discussion, such as sentence framing and questioning, are meant to provide high levels of support as students build speaking (among other) skills. These skills are crucial to students engaging in more sophisticated forms of discussion, like Reflective Discussion Circles (McGriff & Clemons, 2019) and Philosophical Dialogue (Serriere et al., 2017), which require students to share their ideas in ways that are comprehensible to their discussion partners and effectively make content-based arguments while avoiding starting personal arguments.

A variety of structured discussion models enable teachers to be explicit in introducing and explaining the expected use of various speaking skills and strategies (e.g., debate, discourse). Structured discussion includes a wide variety of models, but the common thread is supporting students to be attentive to a particular aspect or aspects of speaking. For example, when using the think-pair-share, students are attentive to responding to a prompt, whereas Socratic seminars are focused on students' abilities to question, paraphrase, and synthesize ideas based on what they have heard. We share an example of a pyramid discussion in the grades 3–5 classroom application.

While not addressed separately in this chapter, anchor charts are an important resource to foster students' speaking skills in elementary classrooms and are mentioned in both classroom applications. Anchor charts are visual reminders that "anchor" classroom practices, thinking, or norms. These charts are often co-created to engage students in the process and make it more likely that students will reference them as they become more independent in their learning (Martinelli & Mraz, 2012; Moses & Lee, 2014; Zoch et al., 2018).

CLASSROOM APPLICATIONS, K–2

As noted previously, most K–2 students will know how to speak. The task at hand for teachers is to help students develop their speaking skills to accomplish particular goals, such as effectively communicating with others, including sharing information and asking and answering questions in ways that can be understood by others.

CONNECTIONS TO THE *C3 FRAMEWORK* AND *COMMON CORE STATE STANDARDS*

The *C3 Framework* leans heavily on standards for English language arts when describing speaking and listening, stating that the *Common Core State Standards* for speaking and listening are essential for many aspects of inquiry (e.g., asking questions, making evidence-based claims) called for in the *C3 Framework*.

Individually and with others, students . . .

D4.1.K–2. Construct an argument with reasons (National Council for the Social Studies, 2013, p. 60).
D4.2.K–2. Construct explanations using correct sequence and relevant information (p. 60).
D4.3.K–2. Present a summary of an argument using print, oral, and digital technologies (p. 60).
D4.8.K–2. Use listening, consensus-building, and voting procedures to decide on and take action in their classrooms (p. 62).

The *Common Core State Standards for English Arts*, even for the youngest grades, include standards for speaking and listening that are integral to elementary students constructing arguments, making claims and assertions, and summarizing ideas. Speaking and listening are intertwined, which is reflected in the "Speaking and Listening" strand of the standards. In particular, in grades K–2, the standards focus on students learning through discussion with peers, articulating ideas, and asking and answering questions.

Standards SL.1 and SL.3 primarily address interactions in real time, while SL.2 addresses listening more broadly. It is also worth noting that SL.1 is foundational for SL.3 and for much of the instruction that happens in all content areas. SL.3, while seemingly simple, is crucial to classrooms functioning in a way that allows students to learn through collaboration with others, which is also key in preparing them to be active citizens.

SL.K.1: Participate in collaborative conversations with diverse partners about kindergarten topics and texts with peers and adults in small and larger groups. A) Follow agreed-upon rules for discussions (e.g., listening to others and taking turns speaking about the topics and texts under discussion). B) Continue a conversation through multiple exchanges.

SL.1.1: Participate in collaborative conversations with diverse partners about grade 1 topics and texts with peers and adults in small and larger groups. A) Follow agreed-upon rules for discussions (e.g., listening to others with care, speaking one at a time about the topics and texts under discussion). B) Build on others' talk in conversations by responding to the comments of others through multiple exchanges. C) Ask questions to clear up any confusion about the topics and texts under discussion.

SL.2.1: Participate in collaborative conversations with diverse partners about grade 2 topics and texts with peers and adults in small and larger groups. A) Follow agreed-upon rules for discussions (e.g., gaining the floor in respectful ways, listening to others with care, speaking one at a time about the topics and texts under discussion). B) Build on others' talk in conversations by linking their comments to the remarks of others. C) Ask for clarification and further explanation as needed about the topics and texts under discussion.

SL.K.2: Confirm understanding of a text read aloud or information presented orally or through other media by asking and answering questions about key details and requesting clarification if something is not understood.

SL.1.2: Ask and answer questions about key details in a text read aloud or information presented orally or through other media.

SL.2.2: Recount or describe key ideas or details from a text read aloud or information presented orally or through other media.

SL.K.3: Ask and answer questions in order to seek help, get information, or clarify something that is not understood.

SL.1.3: Ask and answer questions about what a speaker says in order to gather additional information or clarify something that is not understood.

SL.2.3: Ask and answer questions about what a speaker says in order to clarify comprehension, gather additional information, or deepen understanding of a topic or issue. (National Governors Association Center for Best Practices & Council of Chief State School Officers, 2010, p. 23)

Speaking in Action, K–2

Speaking and listening are reciprocal processes, and, in the context of conversation, they typically happen simultaneously, which can pose a challenge for young speakers. Not only do young speakers need to learn to speak in such ways that their ideas are clearly understood; they also need to learn to listen to others so that what they say plays a role in the co-construction of meaning. This relates to all of the standards above, but hinges particularly on the first speaking and listening standard from the *Common Core State Standards*.

There are many research-proven instructional strategies for teaching children engaged conversational skills. The two highlighted in this lesson are teaching children to ask different types of questions (e.g., Beck et al., 1996, 2021; Raphael, 1982, 1984) and use sentence frames (e.g., Baker et al., 2014; Bluffington et al., 2017; Hoffman & Zollman, 2016). Depending on the question or framing, these questions can be used as conversation starters (or to introduce a new topic of discussion) or to build the conversation.

The instructional outline below is aimed at lower elementary grades, in general. For younger students, you will want to start with fewer conversation starters and builders and practice them for a bit longer before introducing additional prompts. Displaying the prompts as they are introduced and practiced (e.g., on an anchor chart, Figure 4.1) will allow for easy reference to them during lessons, both for the purposes of instruction and as a scaffold for students.

While students who are reading independently will be able to use the list of prompts as a tool as they engage in discussion with partners, small groups, or the whole class, emergent readers will rely on internalizing a smaller set of prompts. For these students, you might consider placing picture icons next to each prompt to remind students of what they say. For example, the "I'm thinking _____ because _____" prompt might have a picture of a thought bubble next to it, while "What does _____ mean?" might have a picture of a dictionary.

1. Introduce the Lesson

Prepare for the lesson by creating a T-chart that is large enough to be visible to the whole class, with the headings "Conversation Starters" and "Conversation Builders." If you are working with emergent readers, you may want to add icons next to each (e.g., the number "1" next to conversation starters and building blocks next to conversation builders). To avoid overwhelming students and to ensure they understand how to use the prompts and anchor chart, it is best to add the prompts to the chart only as they are introduced and practiced.

There are LOTS of ways we can learn about a topic or issue. We have had a lot of practice reading and viewing images and other materials to learn. Another way we can learn is from each other. When you share ideas so that someone can learn from you, it's really important to share your ideas clearly so that people understand what you are saying. That means using a big, clear voice, but it also means choosing your words carefully. When you ask a question so that you can learn from someone else, you also need to choose your words carefully so that people understand what you're wondering about.

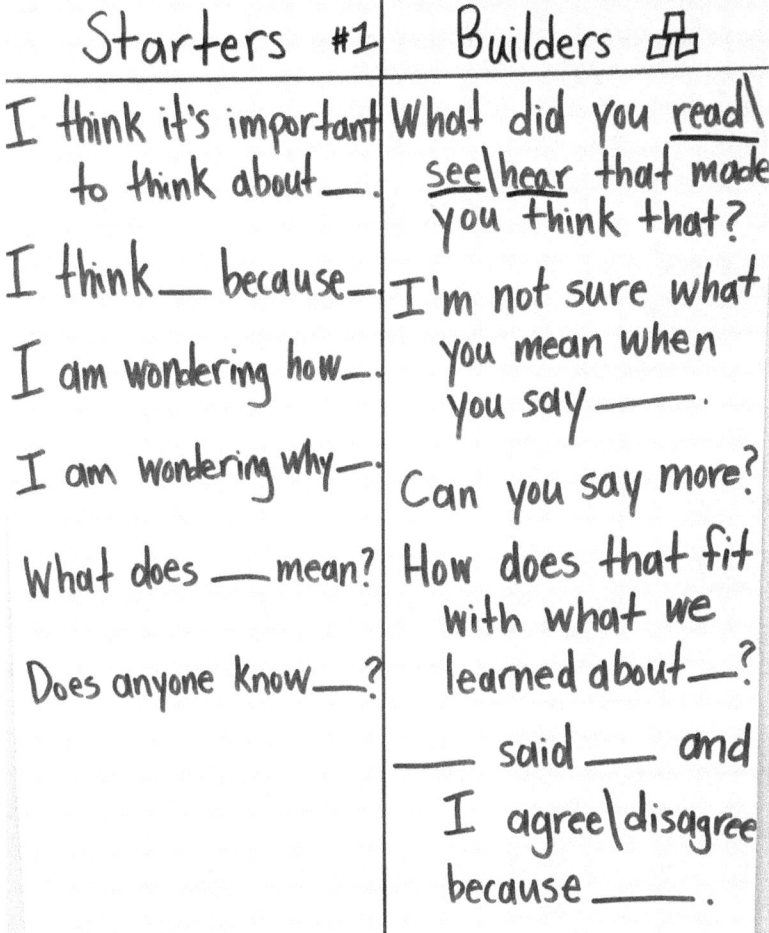

Figure 4.1. Sentence Frame Anchor Chart.

Today, we're going to practice using sentence frames to help us make clear statements and ask clear questions. A sentence frame is a tool that gives you some of the words, and you fill in the rest. Using sentence frames helps us to think more about our ideas because we have to think a bit less about how to share them well.

2. Teach the Lesson Using Research-Based Instructional Practices (here, questioning [e.g., Beck et al., 1996, 2021; Raphael, 1982, 1984] and use of sentence frames [e.g., Baker et al., 2014; Bluffington et al., 2017; Hoffman & Zollman, 2016])

This part of the lesson will build on whatever social studies content the class has been studying. For the purposes of this example, the students are in second grade and have been engaged in inquiry around a "hot" issue: the growth of the electric vehicle industry. Their essential question is, "Is the shift to electric vehicles a good thing?"

Yesterday, we read an article about the growth of the electric-vehicle industry. In a couple minutes, we're going to talk as a whole class about what we learned from that article and what we still wonder. Before we do that, take a minute to turn and talk to the person next to you about those two things: What did you learn? What do you wonder? [This "turn and talk" should take just a couple minutes.]

OK. Now we're going to share our ideas with the rest of the class to remind everyone about what we learned yesterday. To make sure our ideas are clear, we're going to try using the first sentence frame on our anchor chart under the heading "Conversation Starters." When we use a sentence frame, we read the words that are in the sentence, and, where this blank line is, we insert our idea. I'll go first as an example. [Point to the anchor chart while reading the stem.] *I think it's important to think about how much pollution is made by different types of cars. Who else can use this sentence frame?*

[Once students have shared several ideas, introduce the other side of the anchor chart.] *Now, when we are learning from each other, we won't learn as much if each of us shares an idea and we leave it at that. Each of these ideas is a good place to begin a discussion. When we have a discussion—with a partner, a small group, or even our whole class—we have to think about and build on what other people are saying. "Conversation Builder" frames, on the other side of our anchor chart, give us some ways to do that.*

Sometimes, you may wonder where your classmate's idea came from. If that happens, you can use this first frame to ask them a question about it. For this one, there is no blank to fill in; you just need to choose which of these words [indicate read/see/hear] *fits best. When someone asks you that question, they are looking for evidence. When you respond, you'll show or tell them where your information came from.*

Because we're talking about an article we read together, we'll probably use "read" when we use this statement. Let's practice. [Have one student repeat their sentence about what is important to think about. Then, pointing to the anchor chart, ask,] *What did you read that made you think that?* [Give the student time to respond and remind them that they can show a particular point in the text as their response. Practice using this exchange with a few more statements.]

Sometimes, when someone shares information, we don't fully understand. That's OK! That's what discussion is for. If someone shares something and you're not sure what they mean, you can use this sentence frame. [Point to sentence frame.] *It says, "I'm not sure what you mean when you say _____. Can you say more?" If someone asks you to say more, your job is to provide more information or more explanation. I'm going to restate my idea of what is important to think about. Then, one of you can use this frame to ask me for more explanation.*

[Repeat the statement from earlier in the lesson:] *I think it's important to think about how much pollution is made by different types of cars.* [Call on a student and point as they read the sentence frame. When they get to the blank, remind them to fill in the blank with something that wasn't clear. It's OK if you have to pretend something isn't clear, for now. It might sound something like this:] "I'm *not sure what you mean when you say different types of cars. Can you say more?*" [Respond with something like,] "*The article said that all cars create pollution. Gas-powered cars burn gas and pollute the air, but electric cars also pollute the air when factories make their batteries.*"

When someone asks you to say more, they are asking you to tell more about your thinking. In this case, I was thinking about pollution, but it wasn't clear exactly why I thought that was important. When you asked me to say more, I tried my best to explain more about my thinking. [Practice this a few more times, with different students making statements about what is important to think about and other students responding using the sentence frame.]

3. Provide Closure

Today we learned that when we speak, it's important to do what we can to make sure that other people understand our ideas. One way that we can do that is to use sentence frames to help us clearly share our ideas and ask other people about their ideas. When we use sentence stems, most of the sentence is already there, and we fill in the rest with our own ideas. We can use these sentence frames [indicate anchor chart] *to help us share our ideas and understand our classmates' ideas when we talk with a partner, a small group, or our whole class.*

Resources for Speaking: K-2

Student Inspiration for Speaking

Speaking and Listening (PBS, 2023): This online collection of diverse videos, created by PBS, can be used to identify high-interest topics for discussion. https://wcmu.pbslearningmedia.org/subjects/english-language-arts-and-literacy/speaking-and-listening/?rank_by=recency&selected_facet=grades:3-5,K-2&selected_facet=media_type:Video

Time for Kids: This online magazine includes a wide variety of interesting articles to spark discussion. https://www.timeforkids.com/k1/?age=child

Teacher Resources for Speaking

The Big List of Classroom Discussion Strategies (Gonzalez, 2015): As advertised, this blog post provides a big list of classroom discussion strategies, each with information on the basic structure and variations. As an added bonus, you can listen to it as a podcast! https://www.cultofpedagogy.com/speaking-listening-techniques/

Black Ants and Buddhists: Thinking Critically and Teaching Differently in the Primary Grades (Cowhey, 2006): This book focuses on starting points for discussions about diversity and controversial topics with students.

"Projects That Have Been Put to the Test" (Halvorsen & Duke, 2017: This paired article and video describe and provide curriculum for four project-based social studies units designed for second-grade students. While the units encompass a wide variety of activities and instructional practices, there are many examples of facilitating discussion among and with students. https://www.edutopia.org/article/projects-have-been-put-test-anne-lise-halvorsen-nell-duke/, https://www.youtube.com/watch?v=eGWqBZSFgxE)

"Sentence Frames and Sentence Starters" (Colorín Colorado, 2003): This online article provides information on how to use sentence frames and sentence starters in the classroom, including step-by-step directions, tips for differentiation, and many examples. In the resource section there is also a link to an article by Donnelly and Rowe (2010), "Using Sentence Frames to Develop Academic Vocabulary for English Learners," with excellent information on using sentence frames with multilingual learners. https://www.colorincolorado.org/sentence-frames

Strategy: Anchor Charts (Southern Poverty Law Center): This website provides information on how to use anchor charts as part of instruction and also offers several examples. https://www.learningforjustice.org/classroom-resources/teaching-strategies/exploring-texts-through-read-alouds/anchor-charts

CLASSROOM APPLICATIONS, 3–5

As students move into upper elementary grades, the focus of teaching and learning about speaking moves beyond simply sharing of ideas to being more attentive to the synthesizing of ideas. As conversations unfold, students demonstrate the ability to share information and opinions, question one another, restate things they have heard, and summarize.

CONNECTIONS TO THE *C3 FRAMEWORK* AND *COMMON CORE STATE STANDARDS*

Students in upper elementary grades are asked to use what they have learned in order to construct, summarize, and present arguments. The *C3 Framework* invites teachers and students to do this in writing, visually, and orally.

Individually and with others, students . . .

D4.1.3–5. Construct arguments using claims and evidence from multiple sources.
D4.2.3–5. Construct explanations using reasoning, correct sequence, examples, and details with relevant information and data.
D4.3.3–5. Present a summary of arguments and explanations to others outside the classroom using print and oral technologies (e.g., posters, essays, letters, debates, speeches, and reports) and digital technologies (e.g., Internet, social media, and digital documentary). (NCSS, 2013, p. 60)

The grades 3–5 *Common Core State Standards* for Speaking and Listening build upon the K–2 standards, adding specificity to the ways in which students are to demonstrate competencies and tying skills more closely to disciplinary literacies. Standard 1 calls for students to actively prepare to participate in discussions, follow expected norms, monitor their engagement, and connect their ideas to the ongoing threads of discussions. Standard 2 moves students past recounting information toward summarizing a wide variety of sources in a wide variety of ways. Finally, standard 3 moves students toward giving oral explanations of the relationships between claims and evidence.

SL.1.3: Engage effectively in a range of collaborative discussions (one-on-one, in groups, and teacher led) with diverse partners on grade 3 topics and texts, building on others' ideas and expressing their own clearly. A) Come to discussions prepared, having read or studied required material; explicitly draw on that preparation and other information known about the topic to explore ideas under discussion. B) Follow agreed-upon rules for discussions (e.g., gaining the floor in respectful ways, listening to others with care, speaking one at a time about the topics and texts under discussion). C) Ask questions to check understanding of information presented, stay on topic, and link their comments to the remarks of others. D) Explain their own ideas and understanding in light of the discussion.

SL.1.4: Engage effectively in a range of collaborative discussions (one-on-one, in groups, and teacher led) with diverse partners on grade 4 topics and texts, building on others' ideas and expressing their own clearly. A) Come to discussions prepared, having read or studied required material; explicitly draw on that preparation and other information known about the topic to explore ideas under discussion. B) Follow agreed-upon rules for discussions and carry out assigned roles. C) Pose and respond to specific questions to clarify or follow up on information, and make comments that contribute to the discussion and link to the remarks of others. D) Review the key ideas expressed and explain their own ideas and understanding in light of the discussion.

SL.1.5: Engage effectively in a range of collaborative discussions (one-on-one, in groups, and teacher led) with diverse partners on grade 5 topics and texts, building on others' ideas and expressing their own clearly. A) Come to discussions prepared, having read or studied required material; explicitly draw on that preparation and other information known about the topic to explore ideas under discussion. B) Follow agreed-upon rules for discussions and carry out assigned roles. C) Pose and respond to specific questions by making comments that contribute to the discussion and elaborate on the remarks of others. D) Review the key ideas expressed and draw conclusions in light of information and knowledge gained from the discussions.

SL.2.3: Determine the main ideas and supporting details of a text read aloud or information presented in diverse media and formats, including visually, quantitatively, and orally.

SL.2.4: Paraphrase portions of a text read aloud or information presented in diverse media and formats, including visually, quantitatively, and orally.

SL.2.5: Summarize a written text read aloud or information presented in diverse media and formats, including visually, quantitatively, and orally.

SL.3.3: Ask and answer questions about information from a speaker, offering appropriate elaboration and detail.

SL.3.4: Identify the reasons and evidence a speaker provides to support particular points.

SL.3.5: Summarize the points a speaker makes and explain how each claim is supported by reasons and evidence. (National Governors Association Center for Best Practices & Council of Chief State School Officers, 2010, p. 24)

Speaking in Action, 3–5

By the third grade, students (we hope) have had many opportunities to speak and listen in classrooms. However, these are skills that individuals are practicing and fine-tuning throughout their lives, so instruction is still valuable! Prior to engaging in the type of instruction described in this section, if you think your students need reminders of what they already know about speaking, you may want to provide or co-construct an anchor chart, similar to Figure 4.2, on which you identify key actions and behaviors associated with effective speaking and listening.

Speaking Skill	What does it mean? Why is it important?	Example
Answering Questions	Responding to a question with a fact or opinion	Student 1: Why do you like summer? Student 2: In summer, I do fun things like ride my bike and swim.
Asking Questions	Using question words (who, what, where, why, when, and how) to gather information and/or understanding about a topic	Student 1: Why do you like summer? Student 2: In summer, I do fun things like ride my bike and swim.
Deferring a Chance to Speak	Giving someone else the opportunity to speak before you	"I can wait and Anon can speak first."
Providing an explanation	Providing details and examples to better describe what you know	"I like summer because I have more time to do things I like."
Paraphrasing another student's contribution	Sharing what someone else said in you own words	"I heard Zaria say she likes that she has time to go on bike rides and swim."

Figure 4.2. Speaking Skills Anchor Chart.

For this suggested lesson, students will engage in all or many of the actions identified on the anchor chart as they participate in a pyramid discussion (Jordan, 1990). A pyramid discussion starts with students speaking with a partner about a prompt. After several minutes, pairs of students move together to work in a group of four, and another associated prompt is presented. This process continues with student groups moving from groups of four to groups of eight, then to groups of sixteen (or half the class), getting new discussion prompts with each move, and the process ends with a whole-group discussion.

1. Introduce the Lesson

Begin the lesson by reviewing expectations for students as speakers and listeners. Reference the class anchor chart, reminding students about the various ways in which they may contribute in a conversation. Then, organize students into partnerships and display the first prompt.

Today we are going to be in conversation with one another in several different groups. What are some things each of us needs to do when we are participating in conversations or discussions with others? [Take several student suggestions.] *We need to be good listeners and good contributors to the conversation. What does it mean to be a good contributor to a conversation?* [Take several student suggestions.] *In today's discussion, each of you will need to respond to the discussion prompts, and you may also want to ask questions of your classmates. You're also going to have opportunities to practice paraphrasing and summarizing ideas, and you may want to comment or respond to things your friends say.*

2. Teach the Lesson Using a Research-Based Practice (here, pyramid discussion [Jordan, 1990])

This part of the lesson will build on whatever social studies content the class has been studying. For the purposes of this example, third-grade students are discussing their community and have been engaged in inquiry around the compelling question, "What is my community?" (More information on compelling questions can be found in Chapter 8.) In order to consider this broad question, it is important for students to have opportunities to share what they know, consider and reconsider others' ideas, and ask questions.

In social studies, we have been learning about our community. We are going to spend some time talking about what we have learned and some things we might still like to learn. In order to discuss the prompts I have for you, you will need to use facts and opinions as well as listen, ask questions, and summarize what you have heard. To begin, you are going to speak with your elbow partner about this prompt: "Share what you know about our community." With your partner, talk about what you think are some of the most interesting things about our community. What makes those things interesting to you? Before you begin, is this a discussion about facts or opinions? What does that mean?

[After three to five minutes, organize students into groups of four or quads by simply partnering sets of partners.] *I want you to share some of the interesting things you already discussed with your new partners. As you are sharing, decide whether these things are part of our community's history or geography, or maybe another category, such as businesses in our community or "fun facts."* [It may be helpful to post these prompts so students can refer to them easily during their conversations.]

[After five to seven minutes, organize students into groups of eight by partnering quads. Ask students to summarize what they know and have learned about their community, based on the previous conversation groups.] *What are some of the big ideas you shared and, more importantly, you heard from your friends and classmates?* [This is a good opportunity to remind students that they are paraphrasing others' contributions and encourage them to ask clarifying questions.]

After five to seven minutes, organize students into groups of sixteen or into two large groups. With students in these larger groups, ask students to create a list of questions that would help them learn more about their community. There should be questions that include each of the following question words: who, what, when, where, why, and how. One or more students can serve as a scribe for these groups and record the questions, or the teacher, paraprofessional, or community volunteer can serve as recorder for the group.

[Bring students together as a whole class and ask them to share a few of the questions generated in their previous group. Then, ask the students,] *How might we go about answering these questions?*

3. Provide Closure

Today we reflected on what we have learned about our community, and we also practiced several different ways of expressing ourselves. One way we can express ourselves is by sharing what we already know; this is what you did when you initially shared with a partner. We also summarized ideas and asked questions to help us learn more. When we talk with a partner, a small group, or our whole class, we can share what we know—our opinions or feelings about things—summarize what others have shared and ask questions.

Resources for Speaking: 3-5

Student Resources

Newsela: This online collection of high-interest student articles is a great starting point for classroom conversations. https://newsela.com/

Speaking and Listening (PBS, 2023): This online collection of diverse videos, created by PBS, can be used to identify high-interest topics for discussion. https://oeta.pbslearningmedia.org/subjects/english-language-arts-and-literacy/speaking-and-listening/?rank_by=recency&selected_facet=grades:3-5&selected_facet=media_type:Video

Teacher Resources

The Big List of Classroom Discussion Strategies (Gonzalez, 2015): As advertised, this blog post provides a big list of classroom discussion strategies, each with information on the basic structure and variations. As an added bonus, you can listen to it as a podcast! https://www.cultofpedagogy.com/speaking-listening-techniques/

Making Classroom Discussions Work: Methods for Quality Dialogue in the Social Studies (Lo, 2022). This volume presents research-based examples of discussion.

"Speaking and Listening in Content Area Learning" (Fisher & Frey, 2023): In this article, Fisher and Frey share research-based strategies for the development of speaking skills. https://www.readingrockets.org/topics/comprehension/articles/speaking-and-listening-content-area-learning

Wrapping Up

Speaking is a distinct literacy skill that is essential for good social studies. While students obviously are expected to be able to speak, for students to grow in their speaking skills and become successful speakers, teaching must be intentional. The first step in teaching students to be successful speakers is to create space for authentic and supported speaking opportunities. Second, it is important for teachers and students to recognize that speaking skills are tailored to reflect the information and ideas being built upon or shared.

Chat and Change

"Chat and change" topics can be used as a menu of discussion starters for professional learning communities (PLCs), teacher education courses, or book clubs. You can also use them to guide your individual thinking about how to move the instructional practices in the chapter into your classroom.

- Why is it important for students to have discussions with partners? In small groups? As a whole class?
- Your students already successfully use some speaking skills. Which of those speaking skills can your students build on? Which speaking skills might require direct instruction and more support?
- What opportunities are there during the day to scaffold meaningful discussions through modeling, engaging children in conversations, and coaching students in paired and small-group discussions?
- How can we build authenticity into classroom discussions? In other words, how can we create opportunities for students to speak with one another with genuine interest?

References

Baker, S., Lesaux, N., Jayanthi, M., Dimino, J., Proctor, C. P., Morris, J., Gersten, R., Haymond, K., Kieffer, M. J., Linan-Thompson, S., & Newman-Gonchar, R. (2014). *Teaching academic content and literacy to English learners in elementary and middle school* (NCEE 2014-4012). National Center for Education Evaluation and Regional Assistance (NCEE), Institute of Education Sciences, U.S. Department of Education. http://ies.ed.gov/ncee/publications_reviews.aspx

Barko-Alva, K., & Chang-Bacon, C. (2023). Overframing: Interrogating sentence frames as pedagogical support vs. language restriction. *Language, Culture and Curriculum, 36*(2), 1–17.

Beck, I. L., McKeown, M. G., & Sandora, C. A. (2021). *Robust comprehension instruction with questioning the author: 15 years smarter.* Guilford.

Beck, I. L., McKeown, M. G., Sandora, C. A., Kucan, L., & Worthy, J. (1996). Questioning the author: A yearlong classroom implementation to engage students with text. *The Elementary School Journal, 96,* 385–414.

Bluffington, P., Knight, T., & Tierney-Fife, P. (2017). Supporting mathematics discourse with sentence starters & sentence frames. Educational Development Center. http://courses.maine.edc.org/files/Interactive-STEM-Tool-Strategy-Sentence-Starters.pdf

Brugar, K. A. (2023). Everything is L.O.C.A.L.! Making curricular connections that are close to home. *Social Studies and the Young Learner*, *36*(2), 18–22.

Donnelly, W. B., & Roe, C. J. (2010). Using sentence frames to develop academic vocabulary for English learners. *The Reading Teacher*, *64*, 131–136.

Feldman, H. M. (2019). How young children learn language and speech: Implications of theory and evidence for pediatric clinical practice. *Pediatric Review*, *40*(8), 398–411.

Fisher, D., & Frey, N. (2018). Using questions to drive content area learning: Revising old favorites. *The Reading Teacher*, *72*(3), 406–411.

Gregory, A. E., & Cahill, M. A. (2010). Kindergarteners can do it, too! Comprehension strategies for early readers. *The Reading Teacher*, *63*, 515–520.

Hess, D. (2004). Discussion in social studies: Is it worth the trouble? *Social Education*, *68*(2), 151–155.

Hoffman, L., & Zollman, A. (2016). What STEM teachers need to know and do for English language learners (ELLs): Using literacy to learn. *Journal of STEM Education*, *51*(1), 83–94.

Jordan, R. R. (1990). Pyramid discussions. *ELT Journal*, *44*, 46–54.

Joseph, L. M., Alber-Morgan, S., Cullen, J., & Rouse, C. (2016). The effects of self-questioning on reading comprehension: A literature review. *Reading & Writing Quarterly*, *32*, 152–173.

Martinelli, M., & Mraz, M. (2012). *Smarter charts k–2: Optimizing an instructional staple to create independent readers and writers*. Heinemann.

McGriff, M., & Clemons, S. (2019). Reflective discussion circle: A framework for promoting civic engagement. *Social Studies and the Young Learner*, *31*(4), 3–8. https://www.socialstudies.org/system/files/publications/articles/yl_310403.pdf

Moses, E., & Lee, H. (2014). *Imitate and innovate anchor charts*. International Reading Association.

National Council for the Social Studies. (2013). *The college, career, and civic life (C3) framework for social studies state standards: Guidance for enhancing the rigor of k–12 civics, economics, geography, and history*. Authors.

National Governors Association Center for Best Practices & Council of Chief State School Officers. (2010). *Common core state standards*. Authors.

Raphael, T. E. (1982). Teaching children question-answering strategies. *The Reading Teacher*, *36*, 186–191.

Raphael, T. E. (1984). Teaching learners about sources of information for answering questions. *Journal of Reading*, *27*, 303–311.

Rodriguez, N. N., & Swalwell, K. (2022). *Social studies for a better world: An anti-oppressive approach for elementary education*. Norton.

Rosenshine, B., Meister, C., & Chapman, S. (1996). Teaching students to generate questions: A review of the intervention studies. *Review of Educational Research*, *66*, 181–221.

Serriere, S. C., Burroughs, M. D., & Mitra, D. L. (2017). Kindergartners and "philosophical dialogue": Supporting child agency in the classroom. *Social Studies and the Young Learner*, *27*(4), 8–12.

Swan, K., Griffin, S., Grant, S. G., & Lee, J. (2013). *College, career, and civic life C3 framework for social studies standards: Guidance for enhancing the rigor of k–12 civics, economics, geography, and history*. National Council for the Social Studies.

Zoch, M., Davis, S., & Gray, E. S. (2018). If these walls could talk: The communication of literacy through teacher-created talks. *Viewpoints and Visions*, *95*(6), 370–392.

Children's Literature and Lesson Resources Referenced

Colorín Colorado. (2003). *Sentence frames and sentence starters.* https://www.colorincolorado.org/sentence-frames

Cowhey, M. (2006). *Black ants and Buddhists: Thinking critically and teaching differently in the primary grades.* Routledge.

Fisher, D., & Frey, N. (2023). *Speaking and listening in content area learning.* Reading Rockets. https://www.readingrockets.org/topics/comprehension/articles/speaking-and-listening-content-area-learning

Gonzalez, J. (2015). *The big list of class discussion strategies.* https://www.cultofpedagogy.com/speaking-listening-techniques/

Halvorsen, A., & Duke, N. K. (2017). *Projects that have been put to the test.* https://www.edutopia.org/article/projects-have-been-put-test-anne-lise-halvorsen-nell-duke/

Lo, J. C. (2022). *Making classroom discussions work: Methods for quality dialogue in the social studies.* Teachers College Press.

Newsela. (2014). *Newsela.* https://newsela.com/

PBS. (2023). Speaking and listening (2024). PBS learning for teachers. https://wcmu.pbslearningmedia.org/subjects/english-language-arts-and-literacy/speaking-and-listening/?rank_by=recency&selected_facet=grades:3-5,K-2&selected_facet=media_type:Video

Southern Poverty Law Center: Learning for Justice. (n.d.). *Teaching strategy: Anchor charts.* https://www.learningforjustice.org/classroom-resources/teaching-strategies/exploring-texts-through-read-alouds/anchor-charts

Time for Kids. (2023). Articles. https://www.timeforkids.com/k1/?age=child

CHAPTER 5

Listening
SETTING A PURPOSE, STAYING ENGAGED

After attending a naturalization ceremony, Mr. M's fourth-grade students settle in for their morning meeting. Mr M. opens a conversation, linking their social studies learning to the morning's event. "Today our school hosted a naturalization ceremony where we were able to watch as individuals who were born in other countries became citizens of the United States. What do we call a person who moves from one country to another?"

Hands go up, and a student shares, "An immigrant because they immigrated to a new place." Mr. M says, "Absolutely! The person is an immigrant, and immigrate is the action they did. Those words are very similar, but the endings tell us more about what they mean. In the ceremony today, the judge told everyone where each new citizen was from before asking them to take the Oath of Allegiance. I am very excited that two of the new U.S. citizens that were at the ceremony will be joining us this afternoon to share a bit about their experiences. In order to get ready for this visit, we are going to prepare ourselves for an interview."

Mr. M continues, "An interview is when someone, an interviewer, asks a person, the interviewee, particular questions about a topic or experience the person knows a lot about. For example, Fern knows a lot about swimming so we might interview her about swimming and ask her questions like, 'What is your favorite stroke? And why do you like to swim?

"The words interviewer, interviewee, and interview are really similar, except for the endings! The interviewer is the person asking the questions, the interviewee is the person answering them, and the interview is the event, but it can also be a verb—like, 'I am going to interview you.'"

Mr. M displays a bubble graphic organizer on the whiteboard before saying, "We've been thinking about the supporting question, 'What are the experiences of people who immigrate?' Before our guests arrive, we are going to fill out the 'heard' bubbles, based on what we heard at the naturalization ceremony. Then, we will decide on what else we are wondering that we might be able to ask about in our interviews. Finally, we'll turn our wonderings into interview questions. When our interviewees respond to our questions, we will listen carefully so that we can record their responses on our graphic organizer as things we have learned."

68   CHAPTER 5

Pointing to the supporting question, "What are the experiences of people who immigrate?" Mr. M turns his attention to his class and asks, "What did you hear about the experiences of people who immigrate at today's ceremony?" The students share several things they learned from listening to the ceremony. Mr. M adds their contributions to the graphic organizer (Figure 5.1).

"These are excellent examples of things you heard during today's ceremony. Now, based on what we heard at the ceremony and some of the things you learned, what are you still wondering about the experiences of people who immigrate?" Mr. M records several wonderings on the graphic organizer.

Figure 5.1.   Heard and Wonder Bubble Graphic Organizer.

The class considers each wondering and what questions they might ask during the interview. For example, in considering the wondering, "What kind of hard work did they have to do?" they decide to ask, "What was the hardest part about becoming a citizen?" and "What made you keep trying?"

When the class is finished creating their questions, Mr. M continues: "I really like that each of your questions was based on our supporting question and something you heard at the ceremony and wanted to know more about. When we interview our guests, we need to be careful listeners so we can learn more. What does that mean?" Arlo raises his hand and shares, "I am going to look at the guests when they are talking so they know I am listening." Then, Shamus asks, "Can I ask a question we didn't write down if I hear something I don't get or want to know more about?" "Yes!" Mr. M says. "Asking questions about what you hear is a great way to demonstrate you are listening. You could also summarize what you hear."

The students in the above vignette demonstrated that they were actively listening during the morning ceremony and previous instruction. They had great ideas! Because listening is comprised of a collection of skills and strategies, Mr. M also pushed them to discuss ways in which they might be strong, intentional listeners in a new context, interviews. They are learning that listening is a skill set that includes various smaller skills they can enact—for example, using purposeful body language, reflective questioning, and summarization. They are learning that improving listening skills requires practice.

What Is Listening?

Listening encompasses understanding spoken language and sign language, involving comprehension of auditory and visual communication. Just as most people are born ready to learn to speak, most people are born hardwired and ready to learn to listen. However, as most of us have experienced within and beyond our teaching lives, listening is also a skill for which there are varied levels of proficiency.

Being able to hear someone speak or see someone sign is not the same as really listening to them; listening requires intention. When academic listening is at its best, listeners have a purpose that guides their attention, and, in the case of listening during a discussion, they are particularly attentive to what others are saying so that they can consider how to build upon their ideas. Strong listeners can hold on to, but suspend, what they want to say so that they can thoroughly consider what others are saying and how they might respond.

As with reading, listening is about comprehension of language. Listening is also influenced by many (but not all) of the same factors, such as motivation, engagement, strategy use, cultural and content knowledge, verbal reasoning, and vocabulary. However, despite these similarities, there are also notable differences. The most obvious difference is that, instead of extracting and constructing meaning with texts, listeners extract and construct meaning from auditory or visual language.

Listening also presents different affordances and challenges than reading. For example, listening removes some barriers to understanding information, such as the demands of decoding and fluency. However, listening can be more challenging, at least during live discussions, because of the inability to revisit the text, particularly when there are many participants. There is no reread or rewind in a live discussion, which means attention and memory skills may be more important than in reading (Wolf et al., 2019).

As with written materials, primary sources, like oral histories, that students listen to assume cultural and content knowledge that students may or may not have. In contrast to written materials, dynamic sources of auditory or visual information (i.e., communication happening in real time) can be adjusted to accommodate gaps in knowledge. This occurs when listeners respond to speakers by asking questions or otherwise expressing lack of understanding or misunderstanding, which prompts clarification from the speakers.

It is because of these differences that teaching reading strategies is not sufficient to support development of listening skills, though the underlying purposes of listening and reading are often quite similar.

WHY IS LISTENING IMPORTANT?

Like speaking, listening is a key to effective collaboration with others, a core tenet of social studies. When engaging in social studies learning and action, students use a variety of listening skills to understand questions and statements from others so that they can respond appropriately, ask and answer questions, consider and respond to different points of view and alternative ways of thinking, learn from peers and sources, and engage in collaborative civic action. Listening skills are particularly important to inquiry methods of social studies instruction, as they are necessary for gaining access to and gathering information from many sources.

Focusing on listening comprehension is particularly important in the content areas because listening provides access to information in situations where decoding skills might otherwise impede such access, particularly for emergent and young readers. Imagine how limiting it would be for kindergarten or first-grade students to only have access to social studies sources they could read independently! In addition to being important to understanding auditory sources, such as speeches, interviews, and songs, in the elementary grades, skilled listening is essential for facilitating access to audio versions of written texts. (For more on multimodal texts, see Chapter 6.)

If you're worried that the investment in listening comprehension strategy instruction isn't worth the time, don't be. Students develop their abilities and need to use listening as a primary source of information over time. In other words, we are never too old to learn and practice better listening. First, everyone needs to know how to listen to others and understand what they are saying in order to be an active citizen. Second, there is significant overlap between listening comprehension skills and reading comprehension skills (e.g., Wolf et al., 2019). Students who are strong in one are typically also strong in the other or will be when their decoding skills fully develop.

PEDAGOGIES FOR LISTENING

Just as reading and writing are complementary skills, so are speaking and listening—there is no listening in the absence of speaking. However, we have comparatively less research about the pedagogies of listening. Frequently, listening is treated as a behavior that students should conform to rather than an academic skill that can be taught, learned, and refined. As a result, while there are many well-established pedagogies for teaching speaking, listening is something that students are more often told than taught to do.

The lack of focus on teaching listening skills is a little surprising as just about any teacher, any day, will tell you that listening is vitally important to learning. That said, we do have some strong research on general pedagogical considerations for teaching listening skills and listening-comprehension strategies, the results of which are applicable to both reading and listening.

One general consideration is that research supports presenting written text alongside audio material. This isn't always possible because, sometimes, students listen to texts that don't have a written component, for example, a guest speaker or an interview done in real time. However, other times, they listen to someone reading a text or they watch and listen to a video with available captions. In this case, research indicates that it is best that students see and hear the text, simultaneously. This approach has been shown to be beneficial for vocabulary learning (e.g., Valentini et al., 2023) and fluency (e.g., Skinner et al., 1997).

We also know that active listening is more effective than passive listening. Both general engagement and student talk mediate listening comprehension, with higher engagement and more student discussion leading to better listening comprehension (e.g., Lepola et al., 2023). This means that the goal is *not* for students to be quiet so that they can listen more effectively. Rather, they should be engaged while listening through writing, drawing, and lots and lots of talking.

In terms of pedagogy to teach listening, in this chapter, we lean heavily on what we know about comprehension of text, which is often studied in relation to reading but which has close research and theoretical ties to listening pedagogy. In both the K–2 and 3–5 classroom applications, pedagogy will be centered on setting a purpose for listening and focusing attention.

Setting a purpose for reading or listening to a text cues students to distinguish between more and less important information, using their limited resources to focus on the pieces of information that best suit their needs. Paying selective attention is a hallmark of skilled listeners. These students are more likely than their unskilled counterparts to selectively attend to the text and monitor their comprehension with their purpose in mind. This is particularly true of students learning to listen in a new language (e.g., Vandergrift, 2003), but parallel research on reading comprehension indicates that it is very likely true for all listeners (e.g., Pressley, 2000).

CLASSROOM APPLICATIONS, K–2

This lesson is part of a larger classroom inquiry centered on the question, "Is the president the most important person in government?" (adapted from C3 Teachers, n.d.). In this lesson, students are focused on the supporting question, "What does the president do?" They will first set their purpose for listening as responding to this question. Then, as they listen to a text read aloud, they will share what they hear that is responsive to the question and what that information makes them think about the importance of the president.

There are lots of great print and digital, age-appropriate texts on this topic (see *Resources for Listening: K–2* for a sampling). In this lesson, the students are listening to their teacher read the book *What's the President's Job?* by Allison Singer (2021).

CONNECTIONS TO THE *C3 FRAMEWORK* AND *COMMON CORE STATE STANDARDS*

The *C3 Framework* "views the skill of asking questions and the desire to answer them as being so fundamental to the inquiry process that inquiry cannot begin until students have developed questioning skills" (2013, p. 27). In this lesson, students are learning to focus their attention while listening in order to respond to a supporting question, which, by design, is meant to lead to explanations.

Individually and with others, students . . .

D1.3.K–2. Identify facts and concepts associated with a supporting question.

The *Common Core State Standards for English Arts* also combine speaking and listening into the same strand. In this lesson, the instruction is focused on students learning to listen for a specific purpose and identify and record information that addresses that purpose. Standard LS.2 calls for students to listen to a text or speaker and build their understanding through asking and answering questions. For this inquiry, the supporting question was provided and students are working on building understanding through answering it. However, in a media-saturated world, filtering information based on purpose is also an important life skill. Specific grade-level standards addressed include the following:

SL.K.2: Confirm understanding of a text read aloud or information presented orally or through other media by asking and answering questions about key details and requesting clarification if something is not understood.
SL.1.2: Ask and answer questions about key details in a text read aloud or information presented orally or through other media.
SL.2.2: Recount or describe key ideas or details from a text read aloud or information presented orally or through other media.

LISTENING 73

Listening in Action, K–2

1. Introduce the Lesson

Prior to the start of the lesson, prepare a T-chart. The title of the chart should be your supporting question—in this case, "What does the president do?" The column headers for the column should be, on the left, "I Heard" and, on the right, "I Think" (Figure 5.2). Ideally, this chart will be on paper (not projected) so students can refer to it throughout the full inquiry process.

Yesterday, we talked about starting our new inquiry. We're going to be thinking about the compelling question, "Is the president the most important person in government?" When we work through an inquiry, we are always thinking about the big, compelling question. To help us answer that question, we are also thinking about supporting questions.

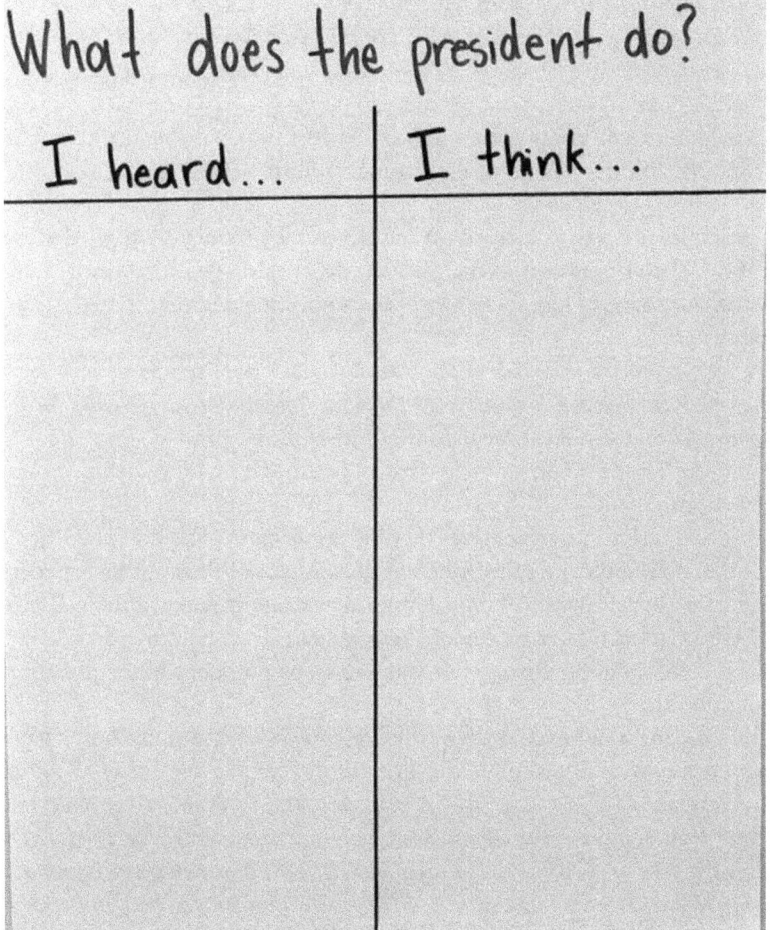

Figure 5.2. T-Chart for Presidential Inquiry.

Our first supporting question for this inquiry is, "What does the president do?" This is an important question for us to think about because it would be really difficult to decide whether the president is the most important person in the government without considering what it is the president actually does.

The president does lots of things, and lots of people have created materials that we can learn from about what the president does. We're going to look at a few different ones over the next couple days because some of the information will likely be the same, but we might also learn different things from different sources. Today, you are going to listen while I read the book What's the President's Job? *by Allison Singer.*

It's important to remember our supporting question while we are listening. To help us keep it right at the front of our minds, I have written it at the top of this paper that we are going to use for note-taking. [Point to the title of the T-chart and read it to students.] *While I'm reading, your job is to listen for answers to this question, on things that the president does. We will stop every few pages so that you can tell me what you heard, and I will make a note right here, in the column with the header, "I Heard." When we're done, we'll revisit the list of things the president does. Then we will discuss what things the president does that feel important.*

2. Teach the Lesson Using a Research-Based Instructional Practice (here, listening for specific information [e.g., Vandergrift, 2003])

In this example, the class is focused on the job of the president, a topic that is tightly tied to the K–2 civics content in the *C3 Framework*. However, the instructional practice is easily adaptable to just about any other supporting question if there are available listening materials.

OK, let's get started. The title of this book is What's the President's Job? *Remember, while I'm reading, your job is to listen carefully for information about what the president does as part of their job—what the responsibilities of the job are.*

Begin reading the book. Every few pages, pause and invite students to share what they have heard about what the president does. When students raise a point, return to the text and reread the sentence(s) they are referring to. Ask the class whether that sentence describes something the president does as part of their job. If they determine it is, add it to the left-hand column. If they determine it is not, briefly discuss what kind of information it is (e.g., where the president lives, how the president travels) and that it is information about what it is like to be president but is not about their job responsibilities.

After reading the book, review the statements and discuss how they might help the class answer the supporting question. *This is a big list of things that the president is responsible for! Now, we're going to take a look at each of these and think about how they help us think about how important the job of the president is. The first "I Heard" on our list is that the president signs bills to turn them into laws. What do we think? Is that very important, a little important, or not that important? Take a minute to think about it, and then turn and talk with someone next to you about what you each think.*

After a minute or so, invite students to share their own ideas or what their partner thought. Make notes in the "I Think" column. Notes can include conflicting opinions. For example, for the statement about signing bills into laws, your notes might include both "This is important because our laws help keep us safe and make things fair" and "This is not that important because the president is just signing the laws; other people are creating them."

Don't be afraid to record what the students think, even if you think they might be incorrect or misunderstanding something. In subsequent lessons, as they learn more, you can revisit their ideas, and they can modify them. This also allows you to strategically expose students to texts that counter misconceptions (e.g., the president can suggest laws to Congress) and supports their understanding that new information can lead to new understandings (the president meets with other countries' leaders).

Continue working through the "I Heard" statements and adding corresponding "I Think" statements. It's OK if you don't finish all of them in one sitting. It is also OK to hold off on some ideas if you know you will be reading a book that discusses them in more depth, later on.

3. Provide Closure

You all did a great job of listening for specific information to answer our question, "What does the president do?" Good listeners think about their purpose for listening because it helps them stay focused on the most important information. In this case, you were listening for information about what the president does as part of their job.

First, we collected all that information by writing it on the left side of this chart as we listened to the book. We were very careful to make sure that everything we wrote down was about what the president does as part of the job, even though we heard lots of other interesting things. Next, we thought about how this information about our supporting question [point to the question at the top of the chart] *helps us think about our bigger question of "Is the president the most important person in government?" We wrote down our ideas about that.*

Tomorrow, we're going to listen to another text about being president and add to our list of presidential responsibilities. We might hear some of the same things, but we will almost certainly hear new things, too. Getting our information from more than one source helps us to get as much good information as we can to answer our questions.

To highlight the importance of using multiple sources, as you read each new source, switch the color of the marker you are using to take notes. To keep track of sources, you can create a color-coded reference list to go alongside your T-chart. Alternatively, you can photocopy the covers of the texts and underline the titles in the color that corresponds to the notes that are from or related to that text, creating a legend for your students. If some ideas are repeated from the previous text, you can simply make a checkmark next to them in the new color to indicate that the idea was also included in new text.

> ## Resources for Listening: K-2
>
> **Student Resources on the Presidency:**
>
> *Eyewitness Presidents* (DK Children, 2021): This informational book includes mini-biographies of the presidents, facts, and photos.
> *What's the President's Job?* (Singer, 2017): This informational book follows a day in the life of the president.
> *President of the United States* (Readworks, n.d.). This online article discusses the roles and responsibilities of the president. Audio and print versions are available. https://www.readworks.org/article/President-of-the-United-States/3096172a-2553-4475-bee4-bbb8b-0f07e7b#!articleTab:content/
> *What Does the President Do?* (Scholastic news nonfiction readers: American symbols; Miller, 2009): This informational book addresses the president's job, workplace, and nonwork activities.
>
> **Teacher Resources on Listening:**
>
> *Speaking and Listening in Content Area Learning* (Fisher & Frey, 2014): This open-access reprint of a journal article contains information on the standards for speaking and listening as well as research-based instructional pedagogy. https://www.readingrockets.org/topics/comprehension/articles/speaking-and-listening-content-area-learning
>
> **Teacher Resources on the Presidency:**
>
> *The President* (C3 Teachers, n.d.): This resource is a Grade 2 inquiry on the importance of the president. https://c3teachers.org/inquiries/the-president/

CLASSROOM APPLICATIONS, 3–5

Learners in the upper elementary grades are fine-tuning their listening skills and abilities; setting a purpose for listening is essential in helping them become better listeners. Often, students are listening for instructions for activities; but, in this lesson, they are listening for information.

In social studies, we encourage students (and teachers) to work with a variety of multimodal sources to better understand a time and place. In the upper elementary grades, students are asked to work with a variety of sources and evaluate those sources in order to address the compelling and supporting questions for inquiry. In this lesson, the students are listening to three different audio sources to glean information from three different perspectives about why people migrate.

This lesson is part of a larger classroom inquiry centered on the question, "Why do people migrate?" Students are focused on the supporting question, "What are the experiences of people who migrate from one place to another?" Students will have the opportunity to listen to several different historical sources in order to answer this question.

Resources for Listening: 3-5

Student Resources on Immigration:

All the Way to America: The Story of a Big Italian Family and a Little Shovel (Yaccarino, 2014): This picture book biography describes the immigration experience of the author's grandfather from Italy to the United States.

Angel Island, Immigrant Station Foundation, Immigrant Voices (Angel Island Immigration Station Foundation, 2024): This website contains a collection of Pacific Coast immigrant stories. https://www.immigrant-voices.aiisf.org/

Grandfather's Journey (Say, 2008): In this picture book biography, Say describes his grandfather's immigration from Japan to the United States.

Immigration/Push and Pull Factors (Scholastic, 2024): This website includes an introduction and overview of immigration for young learners. https://teacher.scholastic.com/activities/immigration/index.htm

Kid's Talk, Stories of Refugee Children (CEPFilmsLLC, 2010): In this documentary film clip, children share their immigration stories and their experiences in a new country. https://www.youtube.com/watch?v=3uoUXlGHWts

Migrant Child Storytelling (Migrant Child Storytelling, 2024): This website includes both written and video accounts of current immigration stories of children from around the world. https://www.migrantchildstorytelling.org/

Teacher Resources for Listening:

Speaking and Listening in Content Area Learning (Fisher & Frey, 2014): This open-access reprint of a journal article contains information on the standards for speaking and listening as well as on research-based instructional pedagogy. https://www.readingrockets.org/topics/comprehension/articles/speaking-and-listening-content-area-learning

Teacher Resources on Immigration:

Classroom Materials at the Library of Congress: The Library of Congress offers a wide variety of primary source sets, including oral histories that you can search by keyword or browse by topic, era, or recommended grade level. https://www.loc.gov/classroom-materials/

Immigration (C3 Teachers, n.d.): This is an example of a social studies inquiry for grade four from the C3 Teachers network. Each inquiry includes compelling and supporting questions as well as suggested resources. https://c3teachers.org/inquiries/immigration/

Immigration Challenges for New Americans (Library of Congress, n.d.): Beyond the primary sources offered by the Library of Congress itself, the Library of Congress provides a full guide for finding additional primary sources in the form of curated sets, online collections, and connections with experts. This primary source set is specific to immigration and includes maps, photographs, and audio-visual materials. https://www.loc.gov/classroom-materials/immigration-challenges-for-new-americans/

CONNECTIONS TO THE *C3 FRAMEWORK* AND *COMMON CORE STATE STANDARDS*

In social studies, listening is a means of gathering information as students engage in the inquiry process outlined in the *C3 Framework*. In this lesson, students will be presented with multiple sources describing the experiences of individuals and families migrating. Primarily, this addresses the *C3 Framework* indicator related to drawing information from multiple sources.

Individually and with others, students . . .

D3.3.3–5: Identify evidence that draws information from multiple sources in response to compelling questions.

As mentioned for the K–2 lesson, the *Common Core State Standards for English Arts* call for students to listen to a text or speaker. This enables students to build their understanding through asking and answering questions. For this inquiry, the supporting question was provided, and students are working on building understanding through using multiple points of view and experiences in order to answer it. Specific standards addressed include the following:

SL.3.1.c: Ask questions to check understanding of information presented, stay on topic, and link their comments to the remarks of others.
SL.4.1.c: Pose and respond to specific questions to clarify or follow up on information and make comments that contribute to the discussion and link to the remarks of others.
SL.5.1.c: Pose and respond to specific questions by making comments that contribute to the discussion and elaborate on the remarks of others.
SL.3.1.d: Explain their own ideas and understanding in light of the discussion.
SL.4.1.d: Review the key ideas expressed and explain their own ideas and understanding in light of the discussion.
SL.5.1.d: Review the key ideas expressed and draw conclusions in light of information and knowledge gained from the discussions.
SL.3.2: Determine the main ideas and supporting details of a text read aloud or information presented in diverse media and formats, including visually, quantitatively, and orally.
SL.4.2: Paraphrase portions of a text read aloud or information presented in diverse media and formats, including visually, quantitatively, and orally.
SL.5.2: Summarize a written text read aloud or information presented in diverse media and formats, including visually, quantitatively, and orally.

Listening in Action, 3–5

1. Introduce the Lesson

Prior to this lesson, students engaged in the experience described in the vignette. The students in the vignette observed a naturalization ceremony; however, there are plenty of YouTube clips of naturalization ceremonies if you are unable to attend one in person and talk with new citizens. The compelling questions for the lesson are, "Why did people immigrate in the past?" and "Why do they immigrate today?"

Sources provide learners with particular information and points of view. Sometimes the distinct information associated with a source is obvious, and sometimes it is subtle. The purpose of this lesson is for students to closely, carefully, and critically listen to a variety of audio sources for specific information and discern the differences among the information presented by the sources.

Yesterday, we were able to attend a very special event and interview new citizens about their experiences moving to the United States and becoming citizens. Today, we will continue to listen to stories, individuals' experiences, and their explanations about why they moved or emigrated from one place to another.

Remember, historians and other social scientists gather information from a variety of sources to better understand an event. These different sources provide alternative points of view, and, as a result, a more complete picture of the past.

2. Teach the Lesson Using a Research-Based Instructional Practice (here, listening for specific information [Gould, 2010; Nokes, 2012]

In this example, students are examining sources associated with immigration, a concept that is commonly taught from a historical or contemporary perspective. Students will explore resources using listening centers and document their learning using a graphic organizer. The structure is easily adaptable to other concepts and resource collections.

Today, you are going to be listeners as you explore three different people's stories at centers. You will be using a graphic organizer to keep track of their reasons. [See Figure 5.3 and Appendix A.] *Remember our prompts: "Why did people immigrate in the past?" and "Why do people immigrate today?"* [The audio for each story can be found at https://teacher.scholastic.com/activities/immigration/young_immigrants/index.html.]

[Directions: After listening to each child's story, document the reasons why each child immigrated. You may use a bundle, bullet, or view for your responses.]

Story #1: Taylor	Story #2: Vandi	Story #3: Sadana	Story #4: Gabriella

Figure 5.3. Compelling Question: Why Did People Immigrate?.

80   CHAPTER 5

Bundle	Bullet	View
Asya's family immigrated when she was a baby because her father got a job in the United States.	Moved from Ukraine to Michigan for her father's job Moved from Michigan to Atlanta, Georgia	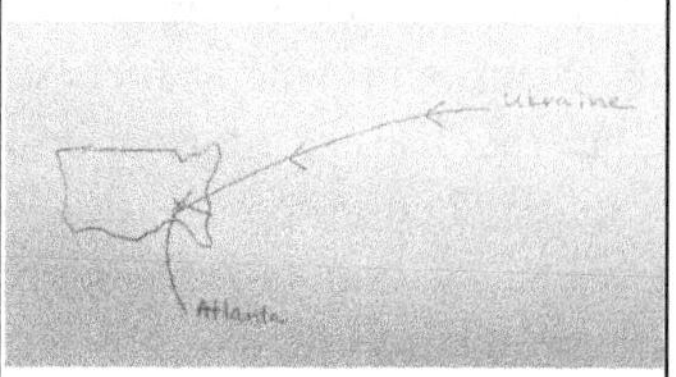

Figure 5.4. Asya's Story: An Example of Bundle, Bullet, and View.

I would like you to first and foremost listen to the experience or story of the narrator. After you have listened to the narrator's story, you can summarize what you heard on your graphic organizer, using bundles, bullets, or views (Vollrath, 2022). Remember, using a bundle means you record your summary of why people migrate in a paragraph. If you use bullets, you will write three or more short phrases to summarize why people immigrate. If you select to summarize with views, you will draw a picture of why people migrate. Before you work on this in small groups, we will do an example together.

Let's learn a bit about Asya from Ukraine. [For other collections of children and families migrating, see Resources for Listening, 3–5.]

Explore the overview of Asya's story with your students. At each page break, model summarizing what they heard about why she immigrated—first with a bundle, next with bullets, and last with a view (Figure 5.4). For the view, think about it as a game of *Pictionary* in which you are drawing based on the clues or contributions students are providing.

Now that we have practiced listening and documenting what we heard that helps us answer our supporting question, I am going to have you work in small groups as you listen to four more stories of children around your age who have immigrated. You will have about ten minutes at each center to first listen and then summarize what you have heard about why they immigrated.

Organize students in small groups of three to four students, at listening centers, and give each student a graphic organizer. All four recordings can be provided while the small groups remain at one center, or students can rotate to new centers to listen to each.

3. Provide Closure

Today you had the opportunity to hear the stories of several people who immigrated to the United States. Remind me what it means to immigrate. [Have one or more students share a definition.] *It means to move from one area to another. Based on what you heard, what are some of the reasons people and families move?* [Students should share several examples from the stories and experiences they heard about at the centers.] *Tomorrow, we will continue to explore the reasons people immigrate, or move from one place to another.*

Working as historians and social scientists, students should understand that events have multiple possible causes and that one experience is not the only experience or the universal way in which something is understood. Accordingly, in this lesson, students should appreciate that the diverse migration stories they have heard make it clear that people move for many reasons, including, but not limited to, seeking job opportunities, being closer to families, and being safe.

Wrapping Up

Listening is a skill set that all teachers want (and sometimes beg) their students to develop. Unlike reading and writing, some degree of listening skills develops naturally, which may lull us into believing that learning listening skills does not require the same level of focused instruction as learning other literacy skills. However, productive listening requires a set of skills that students can select from and employ to meet a range of purposes and that they can adjust to particular content. It is frustrating when students' listening does not meet classroom expectations, but, in many cases, the frustration can be lessened by recognizing that successful listening, like all aspects of literacy, requires instruction.

Chat and Change

"Chat and change" topics can be used as a menu of discussion starters for Professional Learning Communities (PLCs), teacher education courses, or book clubs. You can also use them to guide your individual thinking about how to move the instructional practices in the chapter into your classroom.

- What assumptions do you have about your students' listening skills? What evidence (formal or informal) could you look for to test those assumptions?
- How do you teach your students to listen with intentionality?
- How might you talk with your students about the difference between hearing the words and purposeful listening?
- How do the demands of listening change with the purpose for listening and what students are listening to? What are some examples of these differences from your own experience?

References

C3 Teachers. (n.d.). *The president.* https://c3teachers.org/inquiries/the-president/
Fisher, D., & Frey, N. (2014). *Speaking and listening in content area learning.* Reading Rockets. https://www.readingrockets.org/topics/comprehension/articles/speaking-and-listening-content-area-learning
Goh, C. C. M. (2015). *Teaching listening in the language classroom.* Routledge.

Lepola, J., Kajamies, A., Laakkonene, E., & Collins, M. F. (2023). Opportunities to talk matter in shared reading: The mediating roles of children's engagement and verbal participation in narrative listening comprehension. *Early Education and Development, 34*(8), 1896–1918.

Nokes, J. (2012). *Building students' historical literacies: Learning to read and reason with historical texts and evidence.* Routlege.

Pressley, M. (2000). What should comprehension instruction be the instruction of? In M. L. Kamil, P. B. Mosenthal, P. D. Pearson, & R. Barr (Eds.), *Handbook of reading research* (vol. 3, pp. 545–561). Erlbaum.

Skinner, C. H., Logan, P., Robinson, S. L., & Robinson, D. H. (1997). Demonstration as reading intervention for exceptional learners. *School Psychology, 23*(3), 437–447.

Valentini, A., Pye, R. E., Houston-Price, C., Ricketts, J., & Kirby, J. A. (2023). Online processing shows advantages of bimodal listening-while-reading for vocabulary learning: An eye tracking study. *Reading Research Quarterly, 59*(1), 79–101.

Vandergrift, L. (2003). Orchestrating strategy use: Toward a model of the skilled second language listener. *Language Learning, 53*(3), 463–496.

Vollrath, D. (2022). 5 Strategies to Improve Students' Listening Skills. Edutopia. https://www.edutopia.org/article/5-strategies-improve-students-listening-skills/

Wolf, M. C., Muijselaar, M. M. L., Boonstra, A. M., & de Bree, E. H. (2019). The relationship between reading and listening comprehension: Shared and modality-specific components. *Reading and Writing, 32*, 1747–1767.

Children's Literature and Lesson Resources Referenced

DK Children. (2021). *Eyewitness presidents.* Authors.

Miller, A. (2009). *What does the president do?* Scholastic News Nonfiction Readers®—American symbols. Children's Press.

Readworks. (n.d.). *President of the United States.* Readworks. https://www.readworks.org/article/President-of-the-United-States/3096172a-2553-4475-bee4-bbb8b0f07e7b#!articleTab:content/

Say, A. (2008). *Grandfather's Journey.* Clarion Books.

Singer, A. (2017). *What is the president's job?* DK Children.

Yaccarino, D. (2014). *All the way to America: The story of a big Italian family and a little shovel.* Dragonfly Books.

Appendix A: Why Did People (Im)migrate?

Directions: After listening to each child's story, document the reasons why each child immigrated. You may use a bundle, bullet, or view for your responses.

Story #1: Taylor	Story #2: Vandi	Story #3: Sadana	Story #4: Gabriella

CHAPTER 6

Creating
MULTIMODAL COMPOSITION

Mrs. W's fourth-grade class has been learning about civic participation in social studies. After brainstorming several issues affecting their school and the immediately surrounding community, the students decided to address outdoor safety. Now, they are ready to plan for action.

Mrs. W says, "Class, yesterday we made a list of safety concerns and who might help us address them. Today, we're going to choose five of those ideas and think about who we need to communicate those ideas to and the best ways to communicate them. Let's take a look at our list." (See Figure 6.1.)

She continues, "It's really interesting that there are a lot of different people that might address the issues we raised. We wouldn't ask a student at our school to fix a sidewalk and we wouldn't think the mayor is responsible for picking up trash on our playground, although they might help us if we asked! When we have issues or problems that need to be solved, a good first step is thinking about who can help us. Once we do that, we have to think about how we will communicate with them to ask them for help. We would probably do that differently if we were communicating with students at our school versus the mayor.

"Sometimes, we may want to share the same concern and ask for help from different people. For example, we are concerned about kids doing unsafe things on the playground equipment; and we decided that teachers, the principal, and kids could help solve that problem. Do you think we would ask them to do the same things?" The students seem unsure, so Mrs. W continues. "What would you ask a student at this school to do to help everyone be safe?" Jude chimes in, "Ask them to go feet first down the slide . . . and maybe also to wait until the person in front of them is off the slide before they go down." Hassan adds, "And, if you're on the swings, not to go side-to-side."

Mrs. W continues, "Those are great ideas. What might we ask our principal to do?" After a pause, Zaria suggests, "Maybe she could tell all the rules for the playground on the morning announcements." Royal adds, "Or she could have an assembly." "Yeah, with a dog, like in Officer Buckle and Gloria*!" Nay'la chimes in. The class collapses briefly into giggles.*

"OK, OK. Yes!," says Mrs. W. "We would ask our principal to do things that are different from what we would ask kids to do. We probably would not need ask her to stop going down the slide head first." More giggles erupt, and then the class settles back in. "So, we would ask kids to do different things than the principal, and we would probably

Concern	Who might address it?	Possible ways to share w/ our audience
There are bees in the wooden part of the play structure.	Custodians, the principal	
The edge of the playground is very close to the street and cars.	School Board	
Sometimes we see garbage that kids might trip on.	Kids	
Kids do unsafe things on the equipment.	teachers, the principal, Kids	

Figure 6.1. Safety Concerns Brainstorming List.

also ask teachers to do something different. They would all be working to address the same concern about unsafe behavior on the playground, but we would ask them to address it in different ways."

Mrs. W continues, "Just like we ask people to do different things, we might also want to ask them in different ways. If we wanted to remind the kindergarteners to go down the slide feet first, how could we do that?" Amon volunteers, "We could make a sign that says 'feet first' or maybe write a letter to their class about the rules." "OK. Those are two ideas. What do others think?" asks Mrs. W. Zaria tentatively raises her hand. "Well, my brother is in kindergarten, and he can't read by himself yet. So, I don't think he could read a sign or a letter." Royal jumps in, "OH! But what if we made it a picture, like one of those ones with a red line across the thing you shouldn't do!"

Mrs. W responds, "Those are great considerations. So, what I'm hearing is that a sign would be a good way to remind kids of the rule, but, if we want to be sure all the kids *understand, just words won't be enough. We would need a picture that clearly shows that going down the slide head first is not OK. These are the kinds of considerations we are going to put in this column."* Ms. W points to the "Possible Ways to Share with our Audience" column. *"Once we decide on who we need to communicate with,"* continues Mrs. W, pointing to the middle column. *"We need to think about the best way to do it so that they understand. That is what we are going to work on today."*

What Is Creating?

Form (how something is structured or looks) follows function (the purpose it is meant to serve) and is always considered in context. When we are at our most effective in communicating ideas, we think about what we want to communicate or accomplish, with whom we are communicating, and then, the best way to do it. When we don't consider both the goal and the audience, things tend to go . . . less well.

The definition of creating, as we use it in this book, is broad. "Creating" is when students express or share ideas using modalities that go beyond speaking and writing, typically in combination. This kind of multimodal creation and the pedagogy supporting it are heavily influenced by the work of the New London Group (1996). While multimodal-literacy theory has been around for much longer, the New London Group led the way in advocating for expanding traditional notions of literacy to better reflect modern modes of communication, particularly those used in the media.

While creating as communication may seem novel for schools, it is absolutely the norm in the real world for which we are preparing students to navigate, thrive, and lead. Most news articles, political ads, posters for school plays, directions for putting together furniture, posters for administering CPR, et cetera, include at least written words and visual modes of expression. Many also include QR codes or links to webpages with audio, video, photographs, written words, images, et cetera, which provide more or alternative formats of information. For online creations, the sky is the limit.

Why are so many sources of information in the real world multimodal? It is most likely because using multiple modes allows creators to engage their audiences in multiple ways. This both allows creators to make all or some of the content more accessible to a wider audience and increases the range of people who might be compelled to pay attention. In other words, using multiple modes provides creators with various pathways to form connections between their creations and recipients of their creations. Creators' "reads" of their audiences and their creative choices that reflect those reads allow them to strive for social construction of knowledge, even if the "social" part of the connection is not in real time.

Take, for example, the standardized test reports sent home to families. For some people, looking at the graphs of their student's progress and comparison to norms is a great way to get the information "at a glance." For others, the graphs may be confusing or contain too much information to take in at once, and the paragraph explaining them is a better option. For still others, the two in combination create a fuller picture of progress than either could alone. Whatever we may think of standardized tests and the companies that create and score them, they have made an effort to create accessible reports, and they've done so by creating multimodal communications.

Unfortunately, in classrooms, instruction on creating is sometimes ignored in favor of other skills or brushed off as optional ("Feel free to be creative!"). Similarly, while standards for social studies and English language arts typically call for creation, they doesn't get their own section of the standards and are rarely assessed in any sort of high-stakes way. We mention this because things that are not assessed are often deprioritized, regardless of value. As Dalton explains, this is a "profound disservice to children that we commit when we restrict teaching only to what can be measured on a standardized test" (2020, p. 168). The good news is, it doesn't have to be this way!

WHY IS CREATING IMPORTANT?

There are lots of reasons to invest in teaching students to be creators. First, to reiterate, one really good reason is that creating allows students to participate in the types of real-world communication they see every day. Also, creating inherently involves making careful choices about the best ways to communicate in specific contexts. Choice, in general, is a great motivator for learning (Evans & Boucher, 2015).

Another important reason to foster students' learning to create is that it creates points of access for a wide range of students. The expansive list of what can be included in creating also broadens what it means to be literate, making space for those who may not see themselves as traditionally successful (e.g., Dalton & Jocius, 2013). Integrating photographs, drawings, and audio recordings into communication also supports emergent writers, who cannot yet share traditional writing in a way that is comprehensible to most outside audiences and affords them a degree of independence through multimodal communication (e.g., Rowe & Miller, 2015).

Pedagogies for Creating

One thing that is really interesting about school is that we often show kids how to communicate in one way and ask them to do it in another. In the early grades, this communication often takes the form of showing children engaging and modally diverse texts when we're teaching; for example, the text in Figure 6.2 might be used in a lesson on the Civil Rights Movement.

In these page spreads, we can see photographs, running text, captions, a timeline, a heading, and a vocabulary callout box. There are so many engaging ways that information is conveyed! Great texts aren't just written; they are created. And yet, most often, when we ask young children to share information, we ask them to write a sentence or short paragraph, possibly also drawing a picture to illustrate. Both running text and illustrations are valuable parts of multimodal text, but using each on its own is somewhat limiting.

To teach and learn multimodal text creation, teachers and students may use mentor texts that teach students both how and why to write in a particular way (Laminack,

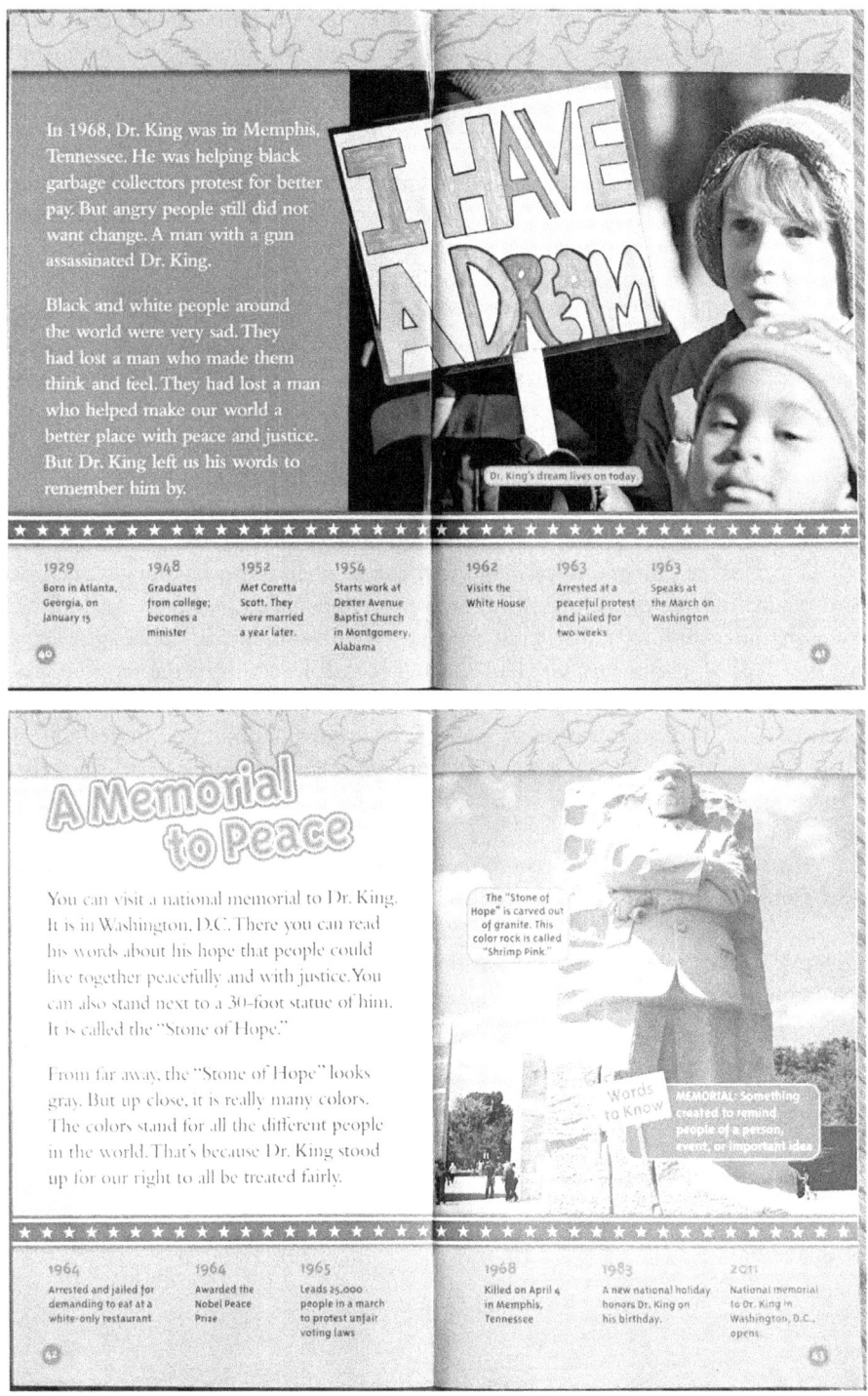

Figure 6.2. Page Spread from *Martin Luther King, Jr.* (Jazynka, 2012, pp. 40–43) © National Geographic, 2012.

2017). Mentor texts are exemplar texts, and using them requires familiarity—almost a friendship—with the text. This is because, first, students read (or listen to) mentor texts as a reader (or listener). Once they are familiar with the book and understand the story, content, procedure, et cetera, they are in a better position to look at the text through the eyes of a text creator.

It is also important to note that using mentor texts is not a quick fix. As with other types of instruction, in instruction with mentor texts, the texts are used to scaffold and teach the creator, not to perfect a singular creation. Using mentor texts develops content creators for the "long haul" (Laminack, 2017). With a few notable exceptions (e.g., Bradley & Donovan, 2010), most teaching resources and research related to mentor texts are specific to writing words, for example, addressing word choice, character development, or organization of ideas (e.g., Anderson, 2022; Dollins, 2020; Fletcher, 2011; Kittle, 2022). All of these are important and also relevant to creating. However, the specific focus on writing is narrower than our focus in this chapter, which is inclusive of multiple modes, often used in combination. Nevertheless, the instructional practices that are described in such resources and research translate well and are the basis of the mentor-text instruction used in this chapter.

As in most teaching and learning experiences, when using mentor-text instruction, gradual release of control is important for students so that they can build an in-depth understanding of how multimodal creation works and of the design choices that best support their goals. Gradual release of control in multimodal creation is often based on the teaching and learning cycle (See 6.3; Chandler et al., 2010; Zammit 2014; 2015). Through this process, students begin by building their understanding of the content and establishing a purpose and genre for communicating. They then examine model texts, compose with teacher support, and, ultimately, compose independently.

When carefully scaffolded, multimodal creation can make communication of ideas more accessible for students in a variety of ways. However, accessibility is limited by the tools available to them and the examples, modeling, and instruction they are provided. In the classroom applications that follow, we share ideas for what providing those supports can look like.

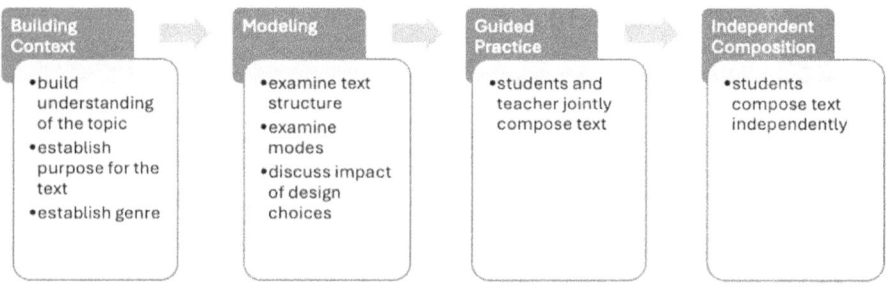

Figure 6.3. Teaching and Learning Cycle (Chandler et al., 2010; Zammit, 2014; 2015).

CLASSROOM APPLICATIONS, K–2

Children in K–2 classrooms are regularly exposed to multimodal creations. In fact, you would be hard-pressed to find a source meant to communicate meaning to students in this grade range that didn't include multiple modes. Sometimes, these sources are so familiar that we don't even recognize them as something to be read or something intentionally created to be read and understood. Viewing them from the perspective of a creator highlights the design features that make them interesting and comprehensible.

CONNECTIONS TO THE *C3 FRAMEWORK* AND *COMMON CORE STATE STANDARDS*

The *C3 Framework* calls for students in grades K–2 to present summaries of their arguments, using print, oral, and digital technologies. However, before young students can do that, they need to be able to create these things and know how to strategically integrate them. Print and digital technologies can be multimodal creations on their own, provided that children understand the possibilities such technologies might offer; oral technologies (recorded or live) provide an additional layer.

Individually and with others, students . . .

D4.3.k–2: Present a summary of an argument using print, oral, and digital technologies.

The *Common Core State Standards for English Language Arts* call for students in grades K–2 to add visual elements to clarify their oral presentation of ideas.

SL.K.5: Add drawings or other visual displays to descriptions as desired to provide additional detail.
SL.1.5: Add drawings or other visual displays to descriptions when appropriate to clarify ideas, thoughts, and feelings.
SL.2.5: Create audio recordings of stories or poems; add drawings or other visual displays to stories or recounts of experiences when appropriate to clarify ideas, thoughts, and feelings.

In kindergarten and first grade, meeting the identified standards is supported by analyzing texts created by others to look for relationships between illustrations and text and to consider how images contribute to meaning making.

RI.K.7: With prompting and support, describe the relationship between illustrations and the text in which they appear (e.g., what person, place, thing, or idea in the text an illustration depicts).
RI.1.7: Explain how specific images (e.g., a diagram showing how a machine works) contribute to and clarify a text.

In second grade, these understandings are expected to be used in the creation process.

SL.2.5: Create audio recordings of stories or poems; add drawings or other visual displays to stories or recounts of experiences when appropriate to clarify ideas, thoughts, and feelings.

Creating in Action, K–2

1. Introduce the Lesson

Prepare for this lesson by pulling together a text set that includes a wide variety of texts that students are familiar with. Some of these should be favorite informational books that the class has read and that have interesting page spreads and text features, while other sources might include environmental print of the types you might find at home, at school, or in the community (e.g., photos of signs, screenshots of websites, food containers, school newsletters, textbook page spreads). See Figure 7.1 for suggestions on selecting sources with strong text feature examples.

In this lesson, you will supply the sources to analyze, but students will be invited to nominate their favorite sources in the days and weeks to come. You'll need both the original source and a printed photo of it that you can add to a class anchor chart. Note that the sources do not need to and should not all be on the same topic. Part of the point of this lesson is that we use different modes of communication to communicate different information to different people for different reasons. The greater the variety, the better! A source that is perfect for one context may be terrible for another, so we're going to need lots of options.

Before the lesson begins, create an anchor chart titled, "Source Examples." You might need to flip the paper to a "landscape" orientation to allow space for four columns: "Example," "Features," "Who?," and "Purpose." Students are likely to want to add lots of examples over the next few days and weeks, so you may want to display the anchor chart in a place where there is plenty of room below it to add additional sheets.

We have talked quite a bit about how there are lots of ways we can learn about a topic or issue. The materials that we learn from are called sources, and sources share information in a lot of different ways. Today, we're going to take a close look at the different ways in which people share information and think about what makes them effective or good at sharing information, who might be a good audience for each, and when we might use each. We're going to start with some classroom favorites and some sources of information you might see at home, around our school, or out in the community.

For each of these examples, we're going to talk about the features of the source (what it looks like, what it includes), who might read or use it, and what purposes this kind of source could serve. We will take notes on this table to remind ourselves later. [Indicate each column of the table or anchor chart as you introduce what you will be talking about.]

2. Teach the Lesson Using a Research-Based Instructional Practice (here, use of mentor texts [e.g., Bradley & Donavan, 2010])

What you choose to share in this section depends on what the class has been exposed to (and liked!) so far this school year. Table 6.1 has a list of possibilities. In this lesson,

Table 6.1. Source Suggestions

Source	Examples
Informational books	• Books students have found interesting, with lots of different formats (should include several examples, each with one or more of the following: connected text, captioned images, diagrams, flowcharts, tables, photographs, drawings, cross-sectional drawings or diagrams, timelines, fun facts, links to more resources, information about the author, endnotes, table of contents, index, glossary, activity suggestions, etc.)
Environmental print	• Food or other containers with simple directions, clearly written in steps • Advertisements for school events • Sign listing rules (e.g., what can go in the recycling bin, city park rules) • School newsletter (often contains connected text, a calendar, a list of reminders, links to more information) • Price or menu board (e.g., from a local trampoline park or restaurant) • Museum art with labels (ideally, from a field trip that students have taken) • Trading cards
Audio/visual	• Student council video news (often contains audio, video, physical demonstrations, print) • Podcast (often includes audio, transcript, and show notes) • Morning announcements • Websites • Presentations (previously given by or for students, which included speaking and perhaps also visuals, print, objects, etc.)

the students are learning about sharing information, so the sources are informational, with some procedural examples, in which information about a process is shared, and some persuasive examples, in which information is shared intentionally to convince someone. Note that, while these examples are listed individually in Table 6.1, many of your selections will include multiple types of communication or modalities. That's fine! You can highlight multiple features in one example.

We have read, watched, listened to, and looked at so many interesting sources of information in school this year, but they're also all around us at home and out in the community! There are lots of ways people choose to share information. Today, we're going to look at some examples that I picked for us and think carefully about them. We'll keep working on our chart throughout the next few weeks, and we'll keep our eyes and ears open for interesting things to add. Let's get started.

Next, introduce a source—it's easiest to start with one they can see, though auditory sources have a place on this chart, too. Have students take a moment to look at the source carefully and quietly. As they do, prompt students to think about what they are seeing.

Take a close look at the example of the page spread, the two pages that we see when we open the book (Figure 6.4). *You may remember this book from when we were learning about what it is like to live in different communities. We all really liked this book and learned a lot from it. I'm going to put this picture of the page spread in the "Example" column.* [Attach the photograph in the first row of the first column of the anchor chart.]

Figure 6.4. Page Spread from Children Just Like Me (DK, 2016, pp. 10–11) © Dorling Kindersley, 2016.

Think about how the person who created this book chose to share information. What do you notice about their choices? [As children share their responses, record them in the "Features" column (Figure 6.5). Repeat this process with several of the source types, listed above.]

3. Provide Closure

Today, we looked at a lot of interesting sources! They all shared information, but they shared it in different ways, for different audiences, and for different purposes. Having an audience and a purpose in mind helped the people who created these sources think about how to communicate their ideas. It was surprising how many different ways to communicate they used!

Today, we read like creators. We thought about what we were seeing and hearing but also why the people who created these sources made the design choices they made. We can do that, too! Tomorrow, when we start our work to share what we have learned about our school community, we're going to think carefully about our audience and what we want to share with them, and then we will think about what kind of sources we might create to do that. This anchor chart will give us some ideas. Also, as we keep discovering new sources and returning to favorites, we can add them to our chart.

Resources for Creating: K–2

Student Inspiration for Creating

Forever Ago (Brains On/American Public Media, 2024): Podcast with great audio reporting on history. Show notes include full transcripts.

The Curator Chat Series (National Museum of African American History & Culture): Short (two- to ten-minute) videos of curators speaking and showing various artifacts to share information about people or events. https://nmaahc.si.edu/explore/stories/curator-chats-series

The Interactive Constitution (Miles & Pinilla, 2019): A great book for Constitution Day! Includes lift-the-flap, timelines, captioned images, Q & A text structure, paragraphs, flowcharts, cross sections, captioned images, and LOTS of interactive text ideas.

Teacher Resources for Creating

"Information Book Read-Alouds as Models for Second-Grade Authors" (Bradley & Donovan, 2011): Brief article sharing research-based practices for teaching elementary-aged students to use informational mentor texts as models for text conventions, structure, and graphical and structural devices. https://www.readingrockets.org/topics/writing/articles/information-book-read-alouds-models-second-grade-authors

Teaching and Learning Cycle: Reading and Writing Connections (Victoria State Government Department of Education, 2019): Overview of the teaching and learning cycle, with particular attention to use of mentor texts. https://www.education.vic.gov.au/school/teachers/teachingresources/discipline/english/literacy/readingviewing/Pages/teachingpraccycle.aspx#link38

96   CHAPTER 6

Example	Source Examples			
	Features	Who	Purpose	
 Andrea / Joaquin (photo spread)	• Photographs with captions, maps, paragraphs, quotes	• Kids • Adults • People who don't want to read something really long	• To share information • To get people interested • To share what something looks like	
 Eggo Waffle Grilled Cheese (recipe)	• Photograph • Title • List (bullets) • Directions (numbers)	• Kids • Adults • People who need to know how to do something	• Show people how to do something • Tell people what materials they need • Show people what something should look like • Tempt people	

Figure 6.5.   Source Examples Anchor Chart; Page Spread from Children Just Like Me (DK, 2016, pp. 10–11) © Dorling Kindersley, 2016; Image of Eggo Waffle Grilled Cheese courtesy of Kellanova.

CLASSROOM APPLICATIONS, 3–5

In reference to the teaching and learning cycle described in Figure 6.3, this example for upper elementary students pertains to the final stage, independent composition. Individually or in small groups, students will use a choice board to select among product options they are already familiar with creating. If you need to teach them how to do something—for example, how to create a webpage—that should be done in a separate lesson.

Most lessons presented in this book are designed to be carried out in a single day. In this case, the lesson application will likely take several days as students will need time to work through the writing process to create final products.

CONNECTIONS TO THE *C3 FRAMEWORK* AND *COMMON CORE STATE STANDARDS*

The *C3 Framework* calls for students in grades 3–5 to present summaries of their arguments, using a variety of formats. As students explore possible print and digital technologies they can use for multimodal creations, it is essential that they understand the purpose for their products and how the specific product best communicates the information to a particular audience.

Individually and with others, students . . .

D4.3.3–5. Present a summary of arguments and explanations to others outside the classroom using print and oral technologies (e.g., posters, essays, letters, debates, speeches, and reports) and digital technologies (e.g., Internet, social media, and digital documentary).

D4.8.3–5. Use a range of deliberative and democratic procedures to make decisions about and act on civic problems in their classrooms and schools.

The *Common Core State Standards for English Language Arts* call for students in grades 3–5 to plan, revise, edit, and produce writing (writing standards five and six for all three grades), with the ultimate goal being to produce writing that is "appropriate to task and purpose":

W.3.4: With guidance and support from adults, produce writing in which the development and organization are appropriate to task and purpose.

W.4.4.: Produce clear and coherent writing in which the development and organization are appropriate to task, purpose, and audience.

W.5.4: Produce clear and coherent writing in which the development and organization are appropriate to task, purpose, and audience.

98   CHAPTER 6

Creating in Action, 3–5

1. Introduce the Lesson

This lesson is part of a larger unit on communities, with particular attention to learning more about the past and present of the community in which the students live. This is an example of civic engagement, which "in the social studies may take many forms, from making independent and collaborative decisions within the classroom, to starting and leading student organizations within schools, to conducting community-based research and presenting findings to external stakeholders" (NCSS, 2013, p. 59). Prior to this lesson, students have taken a class field trip around their community, noting places of significance.

This week we had the opportunity to explore and learn more about places in our community. I am curious about some of the things you learned. More importantly, I am curious about how you might share what you have learned about the different parts of our community with others who may want to visit. To help us think about how we might share information about these locations with other people, I am going to have you look at and listen to a story in which the author, Joyce Hesselberth, takes us around a community with a cat named Sam.

Read *Mapping Sam* (Hesselberth, 2018) to students, drawing their attention to the ways in which the author identifies and describes each place you visit in the story. As students listen to this text read aloud and view the associated pictures, ask them to consider the design choices the author made to connect with them as readers and viewers. Students may mention the pictures and how those pictures helped them better imagine the community. Other students may describe the running text as being most helpful for them to navigate the community described in the book.

2. Teach the Lesson Using a Research-Based Instructional Practice (here, choice boards [e.g., Maloy & Trust, 2022])

Let's think about the ways we acquire information. We might see something, so we are gathering information visually. Or we might hear or read or even experience information—like when we went on our community walk or read Mapping Sam. *Over the next several days, I would like you to take what you have learned about our community and create something to share that information with others. In order to decide how to do this, we will use a choice board. Think carefully about the information you want to share and who you want to share it with. That will help you decide the best way in which to share it.*

Discuss the choice-board options with students (see Figure 6.6 for ideas of what you might include), making sure that they understand what each product is. At this point, if you are choosing to give students the option to work with a partner or in small groups, they should move into that configuration.

Students should be reminded and scaffolded to think about their intended audience and the information they want to share. Once students have selected both their audience and product, they will begin with brainstorming and then drafting their products. (For more information on the writing process, see Chapter 3.)

Create an audio tour in which you guide listeners to five places in our community	Create an interactive virtual map	Create a webpage that highlights five places in our community with a photograph and a description
Using QR codes, create a tour of five places in our community	**Sharing Our Community** Select one of these eight ways to share what we have learned about our community	Write and illustrate a children's storybook about our community
Create a community display	Design and lead a walking tour	Create an interactive physical map

Figure 6.6. Choice Board.

For example, students who choose to create an audio tour will first identify five locations they would like to feature on their tours. Then, they will draft a script in which they will describe each location—where it is, what is interesting about it, and why it is important to the community. After completing their drafts, students will revise and edit their drafts and then rehearse the script. When they are ready, students will record, using something as simple as a voice memo or other recording software. Finally, they will publish the audio tour on a class or school website, in a newsletter, or on a bulletin board to be shared with others.

3. Provide Closure

Over the last several days, we synthesized what we have learned about our community to share with others in a variety of ways. You thought carefully about yourself as creators and your potential audiences. We thought about the ways we can communicate visually, orally, spatially, and linguistically, and you have integrated these various modes of communication into your creations.

Resources for Creating: 3-5

Student Resources for Creating

Mapping Penny's World (Leedy, 2003): This picture book may serve as a mentor text for students as they develop a narrative for a community walk.
From Mapping Sam (Hesselberth, 2018): This picture book serves as a mentor text in which readers move through a community with a cat named Sam.
Looking with Lavar, Kids Tours (Burton, n.d.). This podcast is hosted by Lavar Burton as he explores museums and art with young people. https://mobile.thebroad.org/kids-audio-tour
Explore (Voice Map, 2024): This is a collection of audio tours of large and small cities for students to use as models for their audio tours. https://voicemap.me/

> **Teacher Resources for Creating**
>
> Using QR Codes to Share (Educators Technology, 2024): This website is helpful in considering content to be shared via a QR code as well as in creating QR codes to be used. https://www.educatorstechnology.com/2023/04/qrcode-generators-for-teachers.html
>
> "Guiding Students to Develop Multimodal Literacy" (DeHart, 2023): This article describes the reasons and opportunities for helping students develop multimodal skills. https://www.edutopia.org/article/guiding-students-develop-multimodal-literacy/
>
> "Using Choice Boards for Student Engagement" (Allen & Phillips, 2022): This is teacher-authored article in which choice boards are described. https://www.edutopia.org/article/using-choice-boards-boost-student-engagement

Wrapping Up

Creating multimodal products is both exciting and daunting. It is an opportunity for your students to demonstrate what they know, engage with things they are curious about, and share new knowledge. The wide range of options that students might choose from offer many spaces for teachers and students to be learners alongside one another.

In this chapter, we explored using mentor texts as examples of both individual modes and multimodal creations. Exploring these sources as readers, viewers, and listeners (see Chapter 2, Chapter 5, and Chapter 7) is an important first step toward creating such sources to share information and thinking. Scaffolding students, through building context, modeling, guided practice, and independent composition (Chandler, O'Brien, & Unsworth, 2010; Zammit, 2014, 2015), builds students' capacities as content creators.

Chat and Change

"Chat and change" topics can be used as a menu of discussion starters for professional learning communities (PLCs), teacher education courses, or book clubs. You can also use them to guide your individual thinking about how to move the instructional practices in the chapter into your classroom.

- What types of sources do you currently use in your instruction? Which modes are included, and which might you add?
- How do design choices change the accessibility or effectiveness of a source? How do you or could you talk about design choices with your students?
- What choices do your students currently have in how they share information? If you were to expand those choices, what lessons or scaffolding might students need?
- What is one mode of communication that you might want to experiment with yourself, to gain familiarity with it, before exploring it with students?

References

Allen, M., & Phillips, M. (2022, January 24). *Using choice boards for student engagement*. Eutopia. https://www.edutopia.org/article/using-choice-boards-boost-student-engagement

Anderson, C. (2022). *A teacher's guide to mentor texts k–5: The classroom essentials series*. Heinemann.

Bradley, L. G., & Donovan, C. A. (2010). Information book read-alouds as models for second-grade authors. *The Reading Teacher, 64*, 246–260.

Chandler, P. D., O'Brien, A., & Unsworth, L. (2010). Towards a 3D multimodal curriculum for upper primary school. *Australian Educational Computing, 25*(1), 34–40.

Dalton, B. (2020). Bringing together multimodal composition and maker education in k–8 classrooms. *Language Arts, 97*(3), 159–171.

Dalton, B., & Jocius, R. (2013). From struggling reader to digital reader and multimodal composer. In E. T. Ortlieb & E. H. Cheek Jr. (Eds.), *School-based interventions for struggling readers, K–8 (Literacy research, practice, and evaluation, vol. 3)* (pp. 79–97). Emerald Group Publishing Limited.

DeHart, J. (2023, May 19). *Guiding students to develop multimodal literacy*. Edutopia. https://www.edutopia.org/article/guiding-students-develop-multimodal-literacy/

Dollins, C. A. (2020). A critical inquiry approach to mentor texts: Learn it with EASE. *The Reading Teacher, 24*(2), 191–199.

Evans, M., & Boucher, A. R. (2015). Optimizing the power of choice: Supporting student autonomy to foster motivation and engagement in learning. *Mind, Brain, and Education, 9*(2), 87–91. doi:10.1111/mbe.12073

Fletcher, R. (2011). *Mentor author, mentor texts*. Heinneman.

Kittle, P. (2022). *Micro mentor texts: Using short passages from great books to teach writer's craft*. Scholastic.

Laminack, L. (2017). Mentors and mentor texts: What, why, and how? *The Reading Teacher, 70*(6), 753–755.

Maloy, R. W., & Trust, T. (2023). Women in journalism and media. In *Digital choice boards and interactive learning materials for teachers and students*. UMass Amherst. https://scholarworks.umass.edu/tecs_ed_materials/55

National Council for the Social Studies. (2013). *The college, career, and civic life (C3) framework for social studies state standards: Guidance for enhancing the rigor of K–12 civics, economics, geography, and history*. NCSS.

New London Group. (1996). A pedagogy of multiliteracies: Designing social futures. *Harvard Educational Review, 66,* 60–92.

Rowe, D. W., & Miller, M. E. (2015). Designing for diverse classrooms: Using iPads and digital cameras to compose ebooks with emergent bilingual/biliterate four-year-olds. *Journal of Early Childhood Literacy, 16*(4), 425–472.

Trust, T., & Maloy, R. W., (2022) Women discoverers: A STEM history digital choice board. In *Digital choice boards and interactive learning materials for teachers and students*. UMass Amherst. https://scholarworks.umass.edu/tecs_ed_materials/48

Victoria State Government Department of Education. (2019, December 17). *Teaching-learning cycle: Reading and writing connections*. Information for Schools. https://www.education.vic.gov.au/school/teachers/teachingresources/discipline/english/literacy/readingviewing/Pages/teachingpraccycle.aspx#link38

Zammit, K. (2014). Creating multimodal texts in the classroom: Shifting teaching practices, influencing student outcomes. In R. E. Ferdig and K. E. Pytash (Eds.), *Exploring multimodal composition and digital writing* (pp. 20–35). IGI Global.

Zammit, K. (2015). Extending students' semiotic understandings: Learning about and creating multimodal texts. In P. P. Trifonas (Ed.), *International handbook of semiotics* (pp. 1291–1308). Springer.

Children's Literature and Lesson Resources Referenced

Burton, L. (n.d.). *Looking with Lavar*. The Broad. https://mobile.thebroad.org/kids-audio-tour.

Dolo, J. (Host). (2024). *Forever ago*. [Audio podcast]. American Public Media. https://www.brainson.org/collection/forever-ago-podcast

Educators Technology. (2024). *Using QR codes to share*. Author. https://www.educatorstechnology.com/2023/04/qrcode-generators-for-teachers.html

Hesselberth, J. (2018). *Mapping Sam*. Greenwillow Books.

Leedy, L. (2003). *Mapping Penny's world*. Squarefish.

Miles, D., & Pinilla, A. (2019). *The interactive Constitution*. Bushel & Peck Books.

National Museum of African American History & Culture. (n.d.). The curator chat series. https://nmaahc.si.edu/explore/stories/curator-chats-series

Priceman, M. (1994). *How to bake an apple pie and see the world*. Dragonfly Books.

Voice Map. (2024). Explore. Voice Map. https://voicemap.me/

CHAPTER 7

Viewing

INTERPRETING GRAPHICAL SOURCES

A fourth-grade student waves his teacher, Ms. Q, over to his seat where he has been engaged in an informational reading task. This task involves reading a magazine article about Japan—an overview of the geography, a bit about current culture, and a brief history—and answering a few questions after reading.

When Ms. Q arrives, the student expresses concern that the answer to the question, "What two Japanese cities were during World War II?" is not in the text. Ms. Q responds, "Take another look." Clearly frustrated, the student flips through the pages of the article several times before landing on the page with a map of Japan. As he looks to the teacher, he emphatically points at the text, saying with frustration, "This doesn't tell me what cities were atomic bombed!" Ironically, his finger is tapping text that is right next to a map of Japan, and, more specifically, a symbol representing Nagasaki (one of the two cities atomic bombed in World War II, indicated by a symbol and map key or legend).

The challenge in this scenario was not the student's ability to read the text, but, rather, his ability to acknowledge everything that the text included. He was able to navigate the running text. He was also correct: the answer to the question, "What two Japanese cities were targets of atomic bombs during World War II?" could not be found in the running text. The answer to this question, and many others that teachers, textbook writers, and others ask, are in the materials *around* the running text—the graphical devices, like maps, tables, and timelines.

Viewing

WHAT IS VIEWING?

When considering literacy skills used in the social studies, reading, writing, speaking, and listening likely come to mind, particularly if you have read earlier chapters in this book! However, viewing and creating texts, including multimodal texts, often receive less attention, despite the real world being replete with examples.

It is unclear why viewing is often overlooked. However, when elementary teachers discuss teaching viewing skills, they are often taken aback and respond with some variation of, "Teach them? But it's right there. They can see it." But seeing and *viewing with intentionality* are not the same, and the latter requires some skill. Viewing is intentional and involves making active efforts to identify, observe, and interpret with criticality and a goal of meaning making.

WHY IS VIEWING IMPORTANT?

Visual elements of text are ubiquitous in books designed for children. It would be hard to even imagine the children's section of a library being filled with books without visual elements. Additionally, teachers include materials with visual components in their classrooms and instructional practices (Brugar, 2017). These visual elements are often aesthetically appealing but are also often designed to support and extend the meaning of the written text (e.g., Carney & Levin, 2002).

There are many different visual elements in text that carry meaning. When visual elements go beyond simple illustrations to include words or organizational features to convey additional meaning, they are often referred to as graphical devices. Graphical devices include captioned images (drawings or photographs), maps, timelines, tables, diagrams, and more. Each graphical device is different from the others, meant to convey different types of information and to be read in different ways. Therefore, there is no one best way or even one small set of best practices for teaching about all graphical devices.

PEDAGOGIES FOR VIEWING

Understanding how to view graphical elements of text is just as important as understanding how to read written text. As with comprehension of written text, it is also highly likely that elementary-aged children need instruction and scaffolding in order to fully comprehend graphical elements of text, as their comprehension of them in the absence of targeted instruction is emergent but incomplete (e.g., Duke et al., 2013; Roberts & Brugar, 2017).

In considering pedagogical approaches to viewing, generally, there is evidence that using practices that focus students' attention on all parts of the image or graphical device and scaffolding them to pay careful attention to detail and their own interpretations facilitates deeper understanding. One such practice is Visual Thinking Strategies (VTS; Housen & Yenawine, 2002). (For another example of using VTS, see Chapter 8.)

In VTS instruction, students are asked to look at all parts of an image, graphical device, or object and report what they see or see happening and how they came to that conclusion. Using VTS has been shown to improve evidence-based argumentation skills (Smolkowski et al., 2020), creative and critical thinking skills (Moeller et al., 2013), and skills related to comprehension (e.g., building background knowledge

[Cappello & Walker, 2016]). In addition, VTS instruction has been used successfully as a starting point for critical and difficult conversations (e.g., Gardner, 2017).

There are a wide variety of visual elements and graphical devices that students need to learn to view and understand. In the remainder of this chapter, we first talk about how to select texts to teach about graphical devices. Then, we provide K–2 and 3–5 instructional examples of teaching about one of them, maps.

TEXT SELECTION WITH ATTENTION TO GRAPHICAL DEVICES

When choosing graphical devices for initial instruction, it's important to be mindful that they both serve an authentic purpose for the work at hand and are canonical in ways that will allow you to teach about the graphical device, itself. These graphical devices might be embedded in a larger text (e.g., a timeline in a textbook, a graph in a news article) or may be stand-alone (a captioned image from the Library of Congress, a map from *National Geographic*). Again, the important part is that the graphical devices serve the purpose and are canonical, not what their origins are, as long as they are from a reputable source.

What does it mean for a graphical device to be canonical? It means that the features of the graphical device are typical of most other examples of the device and understanding of them would thus be fairly transferrable and support students' understandings of other exemplars. Figure 7.1 provides identifiers of canonical elements associated with four graphical devices that are commonly used in social studies teaching and learning.

Captioned Images	Maps
☐ Words describe, comment on, or provide additional information about the image	☐ Drawn/Rendered to scale
	☐ Includes title
☐ Uses sentence(s) or a descriptive phrase (i.e., not a label)	☐ Includes labels
	☐ Includes legend/key*
☐ Vocabulary is likely accessible to students	☐ Orientation is apparent (via compass rose or other feature)*
☐ Caption is clearly differentiated from running text	☐ Includes symbols*
	☐ Includes scale*
☐ Caption is near or within image	(*may or may not be present, depending on purpose served by map)

Flowcharts	Diagrams
☐ Images are sequenced to depict stages of a process (with or without words)	☐ Clearly illustrates surface or interior of object or scene
☐ Direction of action is apparent through use of arrows, lines, or order of images	☐ Specific, individual parts are labeled (with or without additional description)
	☐ Lines are used to connect labels to image

Figure 7.1. Graphical Rating Tool (Roberts et al., 2014, p. 313).

When considering a graphical device for use in instruction, these identifiers can be used to evaluate elements that are included and that might be the content of instruction on using the device. Each element helps students meaningfully interpret the device as they are used to access related, but not identical, information. It is not necessary that all elements are included in an exemplar for it to be useful in instruction, but, if only one or two are present, it may mean that the exemplar is not ideal as an initial entry point for instruction.

The list of elements for each graphical device also serves as a framework for teaching topics. For example, when teaching about maps, one might teach about the identification, purpose, interpretation, and/or creation of various map components, including scales, titles, labels, legends or keys, orientation and compass roses, and symbols. Choosing which component of a graphical device to focus on for instruction is driven by the purpose for reading.

CLASSROOM APPLICATIONS, K–2

Instruction on graphical devices will vary based on the grade level, the content being addressed, and any number of other factors. Instruction also looks very different for different devices and aspects of those devices. The remainder of this chapter includes examples of teaching and learning with maps, but readers should note that teaching and learning with the other graphical devices students encounter is equally important.

CONNECTIONS TO THE *C3 FRAMEWORK* AND *COMMON CORE STATE STANDARDS*

In the case of maps, it is not surprising that there are close connections between learning about maps and the geography indicators within dimension 2 of the *C3 Framework*, "Applying Disciplinary Tools and Concepts" (National Council for the Social Studies, 2013). The following K–2 indicators are particularly relevant:

Individually and with others, students . . .

D2.Geo.1.K–2. Construct maps, graphs, and other representations of familiar places.
D2.Geo.2.K–2. Use maps, graphs, photographs, and other representations to describe places and the relationships and interactions that shape them.
D2.Geo.3.K–2. Use maps, globes, and other simple geographic models to identify cultural and environmental characteristics of places. (NCSS, p. 41)

The *Common Core State Standards for English Arts* (2010) also include standards for reading informational text that are relevant to maps. Note that, in the case of graphical devices, because most include both written text and images, we refer to their makers as creators rather than as authors and illustrators. However, the standards separate these roles.

R.IT.1–2.5: Know and use various text features (e.g., captions, bold print, subheadings, glossaries, indexes, electronic menus, icons) to locate key facts or information in a text efficiently.

R.IT.K.6: Name the author and illustrator of a text and define the role of each in presenting the ideas or information in a text.

R.IT.1.6: Distinguish between information provided by pictures or other illustrations and information provided by the words in a text.

R.IT.2.6: Identify the main purpose of a text, including what the author wants to answer, explain, or describe.

R.IT.K.7: With prompting and support, describe the relationship between illustrations and the text in which they appear (e.g., what person, place, thing, or idea in the text an illustration depicts).

R.IT.1.7: Use the illustrations and details in a text to describe its key ideas.

R.IT.2.7: Explain how specific images (e.g., a diagram showing how a machine works) contribute to and clarify a text.

(National Governors Association Center for Best Practices
& Council of Chief State School Officers, 2010, p. 13)

Maps in Early Elementary, K–2

In a bit of a departure from the format of previous chapters, in this chapter we're going to spend a little time sharing what we know about children's understanding of maps and the types of maps that typically appear in sources used by children in each grade band.

There are many types of maps with a variety of purposes. However, research conducted with elementary students indicates that they often associate maps only with navigation—how to get from one location to another (Roberts & Brugar, 2017). This *is* an important purpose of maps, and this purpose matches their experiences. However, in K–2 social studies, maps are rarely used for this purpose. Rather, maps are designed primarily to help students understand human or physical characteristics of an area. The design of a map varies with its purpose. Bird's-eye-view and contour maps are commonly used to explore social studies topics appropriate for lower elementary students:

- Bird's-eye-view (Figure 7.2): Imagine you are looking at a space from above; all the streets and dwellings are seen as a flat surface. The purpose of these maps is to show relative location (i.e., where things are in relation to each other). They can sometimes be used to help readers move from place to place.
- Contour (Figure 7.3): These maps show changes in the landscape through the use of colors and lines. The purpose of contour maps is to help readers note these changes (e.g., between land and water).

108   CHAPTER 7

Figure 7.2   Bird's Eye View Map from *Mapping Penny's World* (Leedy, 2003).

Figure 7.3.   Contour Map, *World Topographical Map* (xingmin07, 2012).

Viewing in Action, K–2

In this lesson, students carefully examine three maps to identify features and infer possible purposes for each. Typically, students learn about maps (and other graphical devices) in the context of content-based social studies learning. However, it can be helpful to provide an introductory lesson in which students have the opportunity to acquire foundational knowledge of the device before being asked to use the device to gain access to content-based information.

1. Introduce the Lesson

Place three maps in a place where students can clearly see them. The maps should be of different types; ideally, a bird's-eye-view map, a contour map, and one of a GPS sort that students might frequently see in a car or on a family member's phone when traveling.

Take a close look at these three images. These are maps. A map is an image of an area or part of an area that has been shrunken down to be small enough to fit on a page or a screen. Maps include special features that help us read and understand them, which we will be learning about. Not all maps are the same!

We use maps for all different reasons; and a map that is good for one purpose may not work for another. Today, we're going to look at different maps and think about what they could be used for. We will also consider how the people who created them made design choices to support their purposes.

Your students may already know the term "cartographer." If not, this would be a good time to explain that a cartographer is a person who creates maps.

2. Teach the Lesson Using a Research-Based Instructional Practice (here, Visual Thinking Strategies [Housen & Yenawine, 2002; Dabney et al., 2015])

The goal of VTS instruction is to have students purposefully and carefully look at each part of an image (here, a map) and think about what they are seeing and what it might mean. Typically, VTS involves taking time to quietly look at a photograph or piece of art and ask the following: "What is happening here?"; "What do you see that tells you that?"; and "What more can you see?" The questions suggested below have been modified to be appropriate for maps.

Take a look at this first map. We aren't going to talk about it just yet; we're just going to look at it carefully. Look at the middle of the map. [Point and pause.] *Look at all four sides.* [Point and pause.] *Be sure to look at the top, the bottom, and all four corners.* [Pause and give students time to look. You may also choose to have students share one observation with a partner.] *What can you learn from this map?* [Have students identify the purpose of the map.] *What do you see that is telling you that?* [Have students use evidence to support a claim.] *What else can we see?* [Have students identify features on or characteristics of the map.]

Repeat this process for all three maps, taking brief notes as you go. If you are showing large, paper copies, you may want to mount them on poster paper or a whiteboard so that you can scribe students' ideas right next to the maps. If you are projecting from a computer file, you can keep notes for each in a Word document or the like.

After looking at all three maps, guide students in a discussion that allows them to compare and contrast the maps, highlighting their different purposes and designs. Ask questions such as, "Why do you think people might have created this map?"; "When would you use it?"; and "What do you see that the people who made this map did or included to make it really useful for that purpose?" Repeat this process for all three maps.

3. Provide Closure

Today we looked at three different maps. We thought about them carefully, particularly what we saw in each, how they were the same as and different from each other, and what each map might be used for. When people make maps, they always have a purpose. The purpose is something they are trying to help the map reader understand or do. Not all maps are the same. Mapmakers include certain elements to make maps good for different purposes. For example, in these maps, we saw . . . [fill in elements your students noticed and what meaning they conveyed].

Resources for Viewing: K–2

Student Resources for Maps:

Follow that Map! A First Book of Mapping Skills (Ritchie, 2009): In this interactive picture book, students learn about key mapping concepts as they follow the characters on a search for their pets.

Mapping Penny's World (Leedy, 2003): In this narrative picture book, a young girl maps her world from the perspective of her dog.

Maps (Mizielinska & Mizielinski, 2013): This beautifully illustrated atlas features maps with illustrations of historical and cultural information about countries on each continent.

Teacher Resources for Viewing:

National Archives Analysis Tools (National Archives, n.d.): These kid-friendly tools provide discussion prompts related to various viewing sources (e.g., maps, photographs, artwork, artifacts). The tools are PDFs that you can print or type directly into. https://www.archives.gov/education/lessons/worksheets

Google Geo Tools (Google, n.d.): This resource collection includes a tool for creating multimodal map projects and an interactive viewer for satellite data. https://www.google.com/earth/education/

Maps from the World Digital Library (Library of Congress, n.d.): This primary source set includes maps from all over the world and various time periods. There are also links to a teacher's guide and analysis tool. https://www.loc.gov/classroom-materials/maps-from-the-world-digital-library/

National Geographic Classroom Map (National Geographic, n.d.): This resource includes a lesson plan to guide students through a discussion exploring a classroom map, as well as a link to a lesson plan in which students create their own maps of their classrooms. https://education.nationalgeographic.org/resource/classroom-map/

CLASSROOM APPLICATIONS, 3–5

As noted above, instruction on graphical devices will vary based on the age of your students, the content being addressed, and any number of other factors. For this reason, though the grades 3–5 instructional ideas we share here are also about maps, the standards addressed denote a more sophisticated understanding of maps and the ways students may use them in various contexts.

CONNECTIONS TO THE *C3 FRAMEWORK* AND *COMMON CORE STATE STANDARDS*

As in the K–2 grade band, the geography indicators within dimension 2 of the *C3 Framework*, "Applying Disciplinary Tools and Concepts," particularly the following, are most relevant to our work with maps:

Individually and with others, students . . .

D2.Geo.1.3–5. Construct maps and other graphic representations of both familiar and unfamiliar places.

D2.Geo.2.3–5. Use maps, satellite images, photographs, and other representations to explain relationships between the locations of places and regions and their environmental characteristics.

D2.Geo.3.3–5. Use maps of different scales to describe the locations of cultural and environmental characteristics.

(NCSS, p. 41)

As in K–2, the most relevant *Common Core State Standards for English Arts* include the following standards for reading informational text (here, maps are the text).

R.IT.3.1: Ask and answer questions to demonstrate understanding of text, referring explicitly to the text as the basis for the answers.

R.IT.4.1: Refer to details and examples in a text when explaining what the text says explicitly and when drawing inferences from the text.

R.IT.5.1: Quote accurately from a text when explaining what the text says explicitly and when drawing inferences from the text.

R.IT.3.7: Use information gained from illustrations (e.g., maps, photographs) and the words in a text to demonstrate understanding of the text (e.g., where, when, why, and how key events occur).

R.IT.4.7: Interpret information presented visually, orally, or quantitatively (e.g., in charts, graphs, diagrams, timelines, animations, or interactive elements on Web pages) and explain how the information contributes to an understanding of the text in which it appears.

R.IT.5.7: Draw on information from multiple print or digital sources, demonstrating the ability to locate an answer to a question quickly or to solve a problem efficiently.

R.IT.3.9: Compare and contrast the most important points and key details presented in two texts on the same topic.

R.IT.4.9: Integrate information from two texts on the same topic in order to write or speak about the subject knowledgeably.

R.IT.5.9: Integrate information from several texts on the same topic in order to write or speak about the subject knowledgeably.

R.IT.3.10: By the end of the year, read and comprehend informational texts, including history/social studies, science, and technical texts, at the high end of the grades 2–3 text complexity band independently and proficiently.

R.IT.4.10: By the end of year, read and comprehend informational texts, including history/social studies, science, and technical texts, in the grades 4–5 text complexity band proficiently, with scaffolding as needed at the high end of the range.

R.IT.5.10: By the end of the year, read and comprehend informational texts, including history/social studies, science, and technical texts, at the high end of the grades 4–5 text complexity band independently and proficiently.

(National Governors Association Center for Best Practices & Council of Chief State School Officers, p. 14)

Maps in Later Elementary, 3–5

Once students are in later elementary grades, they are more likely to have some awareness of the types of maps used in social studies instruction (Roberts & Brugar, 2014). However, if some students do not, then this would be a good time to review them, using a lesson similar to the K–2 lesson, above. You might also introduce an additional map type, panoramic maps.

While the types of maps used in 3–5 classrooms are typically similar to those used in K–2 classrooms, they tend to have more detail and lessons about using them tend to have more pointed connections to what students are learning within the various domains of social studies (civics, geography, history, economics), as opposed to being introductions to maps, themselves.

There are, of course, many topics addressed in these grades, and many maps that could support instruction. Below, we share examples focused on the American Revolution.

- Bird's-eye-view (Figure 7.4): This bird's-eye-view map comes from the Library of Congress's American Revolution and Its Era collection. It is designed primarily to show the relative locations of the British and Americans during the Battle of Bunker Hill (historically identified as Bunkers Hill) (Burgoyne et al., 1775). (See above for a general description of bird's-eye-view maps.)

The example above (Figure 7.5) comes from the Ladies of Mount Vernon Association and shows the New York Campaign of the American Revolution. It is also a bird's-eye-view map, with greater detail than the map on page 113.

- Contour (Figure 7.6): This contour map comes from the Library of Congress and depicts the Battle of Long Island. (See above for a general description of contour maps.)
- Panoramic (Figure 7.7): These maps take into account aspects of both bird's-eye-view maps and contour maps. They are artistic renderings that show human and natural features in relation to one another. In this case, the map shows an artist's interpretation of the Battle of Long Island, noting the numbers and formation of the soldiers in relation to one another as well as the relative location of the battle to the water and town (indicated by buildings). In addition, viewers may notice the subtle incline (or contour) of the land on the left side of the image.

VIEWING 113

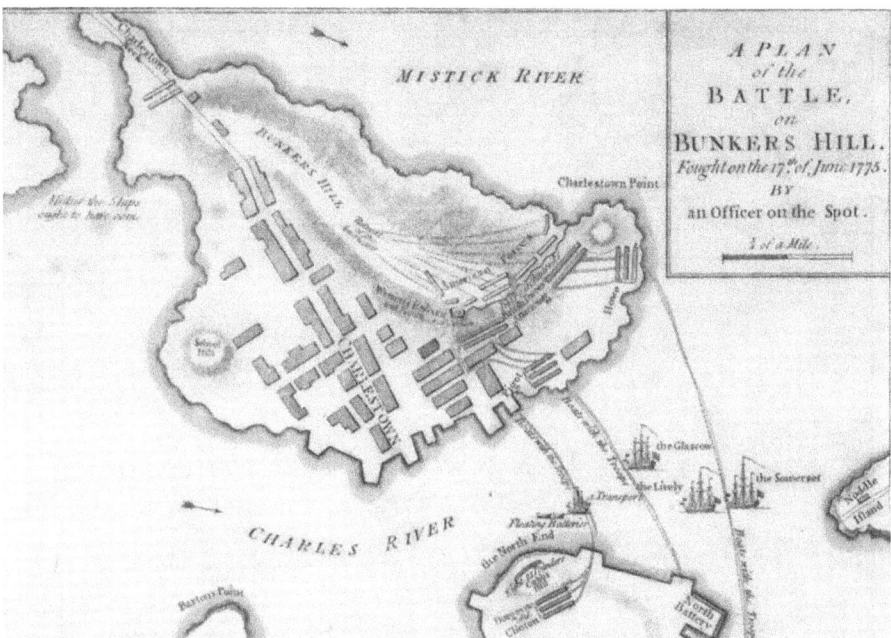

Figure 7.4. Bird's Eye View Map, *Map on the Battle of Bunkers Hill* (Burgoyne et al., 1775).

Viewing in Action, 3–5

In this lesson, we use an excellent resource from the Library of Congress (n.d.), the *Teacher's Guide: Analyzing Maps* (Appendix A). This tool guides map viewers through a process of questioning text (here, maps) in order to build deeper comprehension (e.g., Fisher & Frey, 2018; Joseph et al., 2015). While the example shared here is meant to support thinking critically about and learning with maps, the Library of Congress provides similar guides for other sources (e.g., motion pictures, charts and graphs, oral histories, printed texts, photographs), and we love them all.

The Library of Congress guides are observational tools meant to guide students as they engage with a variety of sources. There are three types of prompts included. "Observe" prompts are designed to help students identify and note details. "Reflect" prompts guide students to come up with and test their own hypotheses. "Question" prompts, not surprisingly, support students to ask questions, ideally ones that lead to further observation and reflection. The prompts do not need to be used in any particular order, and use of one tends to naturally lead to use of another. In the example below, we use the American Revolution as content context, but many other topics would work just as well.

1. Introduce the Lesson

Place the first of three maps that are related to a social studies topic that students are currently studying in a place where students can clearly see it (e.g., projected on a screen). The set of maps should include at least two of the three types described above but might include all three if relevant maps of each type are available.

114   CHAPTER 7

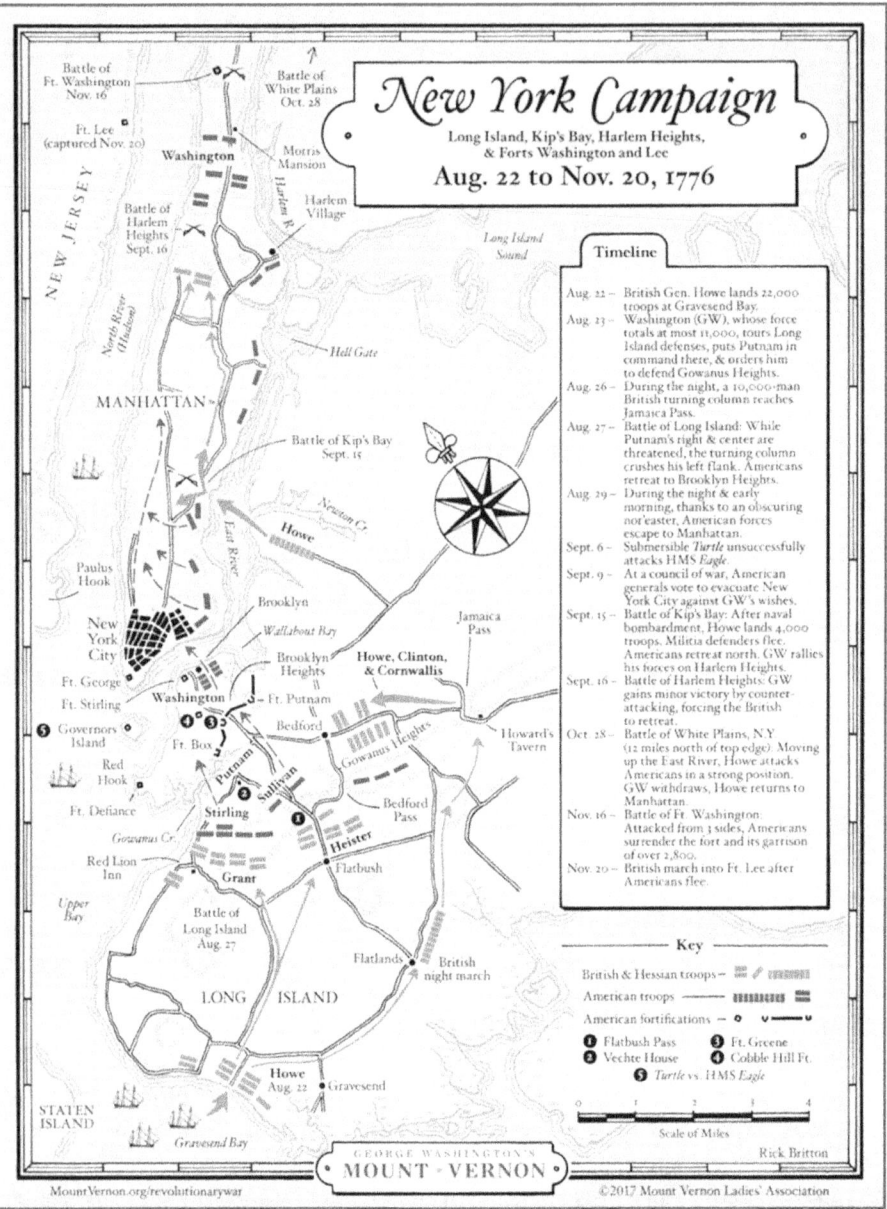

Figure 7.5. Bird's Eye View Map, *The New York Campaign* (Britton, n.d.), © Mount Vernon Ladies Association, 2017.

We have been learning about the American Revolution, using lots of different sources. We have used our textbook, videos, letters, pictures, and lots of other sources. Today, we're going to think about how maps can help us better understand the American Revolution. If you look at a map as if it is a picture, you will miss a lot of information! Today, we're going to look at some maps and ask ourselves questions to help us think about the maps carefully and learn from them.

VIEWING   115

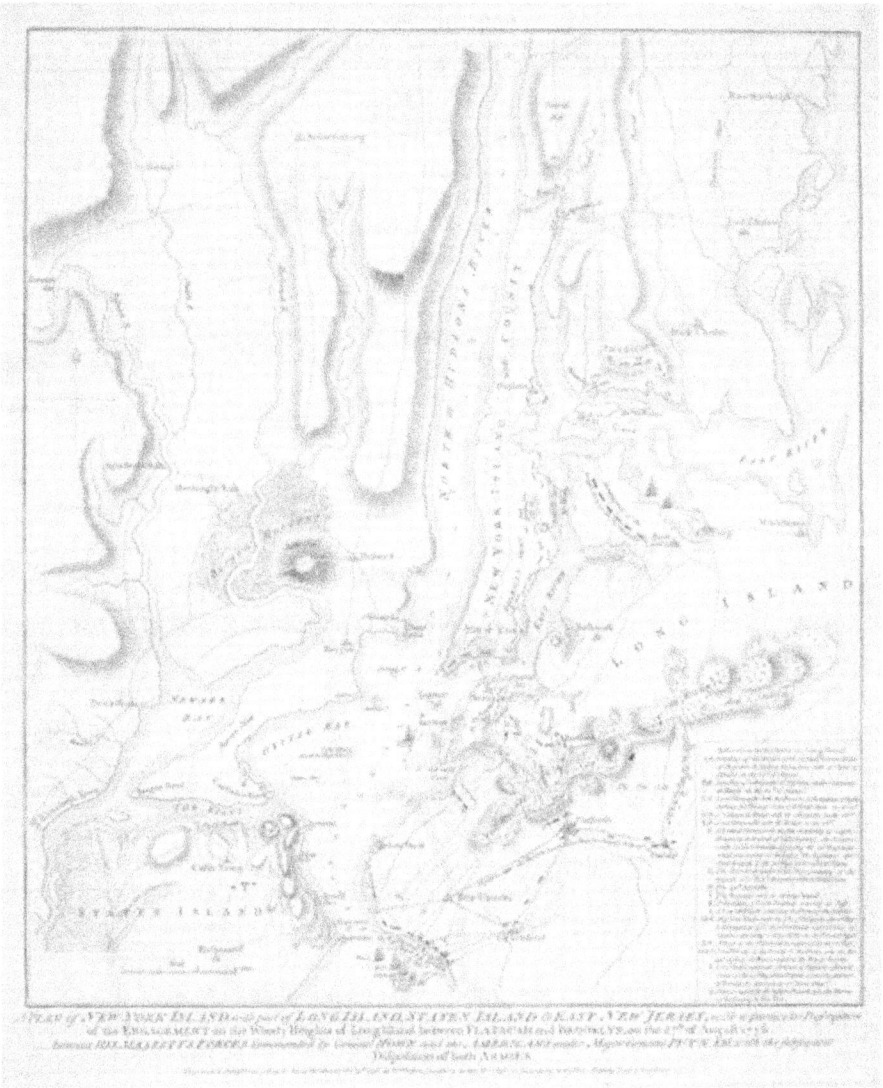

Figure 7.6.   Contour Map, *Long Island, New York and Staten Island, 1776* (Faden, 1776).

2. Teach the Lesson Using a Research-Based Instructional Resource (here, *Teacher's Guide: Analyzing Maps* [Library of Congress, n.d.])

The Library of Congress guide is meant to be used as a tool to help students investigate a map as a source. As a reminder, the prompts can be used in any order.

Take a close look at this map [Figure 7.4]. *This map is from the Library of Congress, and it shows the Battle of Long Island. Take about one minute to look at it very carefully on your own. Look all around the map—top, bottom, middle, corners, edges. Look at the colors, lines, and features.* [Provide about a minute for this viewing.]

116   CHAPTER 7

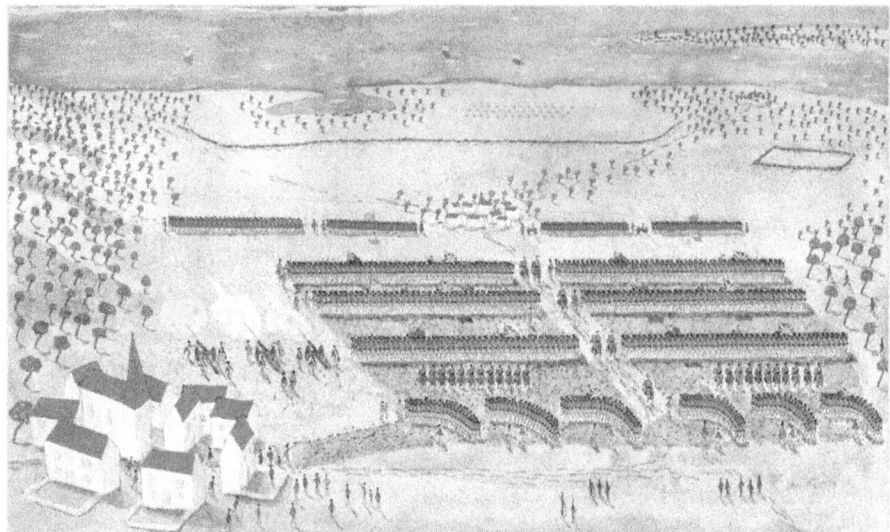

The British attack: Battle of Long Island on 27th August 1776 in the American Revolutionary War: picture by John Fawkes

Figure 7.7. Panoramic Map, Map of Battle of Long Island (Fawkes, 1776).

At this point, choose any of the questions in the teaching guide to begin a conversation. The first couple of prompts in any category work well as starting points. Typically, the prompts follow each other naturally, but having the guide nearby for discussion ideas can be helpful if the conversation falters. If students are familiar with the tool, this part of the lesson can also be done in small groups.

Repeat this process, using the other maps. Note that, if students are new at the process or just very engaged, you may want to spread this part of the activity over more than one lesson. After exploring each map, discuss how the answers to the prompts were the same and different and how differences in the design of the maps changed how they thought about the maps and the battle and what they were able to learn. Wrap up the lesson by discussing when each type of map might be most useful.

3. Provide Closure

Today we looked at several different maps that were pretty different from each other, but all included lots of details that helped us think about the battles of the American Revolution and understand them better. How did carefully looking at these maps change or add to your understanding of the American Revolution? What do you think the person who made these maps wanted to be sure you know? What, specifically, did you see or think about that helped you better understand the maps or the battles?

As we keep learning about the American Revolution, we're going to look at more maps. As we view and observe, continue to think about what the mapmaker was trying to communicate or share about the American Revolution and how that helps us better understand what was happening and why.

> ## Resources for Viewing: 3-5
>
> **Student Resources for Viewing:**
>
> *Nathan Hale's Hazardous Tales* (Hale, book series): Series of graphic novels in which Nathan Hale (the creator) shares stories rooted in familiar and less familiar historical events.
>
> *Google Earth Education* (Google, 2024): Access to Google Earth and supporting geographic resources for students and teachers to use to explore the world in geospatial ways. https://www.google.com/earth/education/
>
> **Teacher Resources for Viewing:**
>
> *Classroom Materials at the Library of Congress* (Library of Congress, n.d.): The Library of Congress offers a wide variety of primary source sets that you can search by keyword or browse by topic, era, or recommended grade level. https://www.loc.gov/classroom-materials/
>
> *Google Earth Education* (Google, 2024): Access to Google Earth and supporting geographic resources for students and teachers to explore the world in geospatial ways. https://www.google.com/earth/education/
>
> *Library of Congress: Finding Primary Sources* (Library of Congress, n.d.): Beyond the primary sources offered by the Library of Congress itself, the Library of Congress provides a full guide for finding additional primary sources in the form of curated sets, online collections, and connections with experts. https://www.loc.gov/programs/teachers/getting-started-with-primary-sources/finding/

Wrapping Up

Viewing images and graphical devices is different from reading and processing written texts and, as such, requires particular skills, both for teaching and learning. In this chapter, we shared examples related to one graphical device, maps. The first step in teaching students to make meaning with maps is to help them understand that maps require careful viewing; they are not purely decorative, and viewing them cannot be skipped. Students need to build habits of identifying, observing, and critically interpreting maps and all graphical devices with the goal of making meaning relevant to their purpose. These skills are not innate but can definitely be taught!

The key ideas in this chapter, as well as those in previous chapters, are useful in thinking about different ways for students and teachers both to access and create social studies content. Chapter 8 addresses how all six literacy domains work in concert to support the inquiry process.

Chat and Change

"Chat and change" topics can be used as a menu of discussion starters for Professional Learning Communities (PLCs), teacher education courses, or book clubs. You can also use them to guide your individual thinking about how to move the instructional practices in the chapter into your classroom.

- What is the difference between seeing something and skillfully viewing it?
- What types of multimodal texts or text elements do you share with students or do students encounter during social studies teaching and learning? How do you teach students to critically view them?
- What challenges have you experienced when using graphics with students? What benefits have you seen when using graphics with your students?
- What opportunities exist (or could be created) to support students to view materials as historians, economists, geographers, citizens?
- What visuals are you excited to explore and share with your students? Why?

References

Brugar, K. A. (2017). "We don't have students color maps anymore . . ." A survey of social studies teachers' use of visual materials. *Journal of Visual Literacy, 36*(3–4), 142–163. doi: http://dx.doi.org/10.1080/1051144X.2017.1397380

Cappello, M., & Walker, N. T. (2016). Visual thinking strategies: Teachers' reflections on closely reading complex visual texts within the disciplines. *The Reading Teacher, 70*(3), 317–325.

Carney, R. N., & Levin, J. R. (2002). Pictorial illustrations *still* improve students' learning from text. *Educational Psychology Review, 14*(1), 5–26.

Council of Chief State School Officers. (2012). *Vision for the college, career and civic life (C3) framework for inquiry in social studies state standards.* Washington, DC: Authors.

Dabney, H., Miller, A., & Yenawine, P. (2015). Understanding visual literacy: The visual thinking strategies approach. In D. M. Baylen & A. D'Alba (Eds.), *Essentials of teaching and integrating visual and media literacy.* Springer. https://doi.org/10.1007/978-3-319-05837-5_3

Duke, N. K., Halladay, J. L., & Roberts, K. L. (2013). Reading standards for informational text. In L. M. Morrow, T. Shanahan, & K. K. Wixson (Eds.), *Teaching with the Common Core Standards for English Language Arts: What educators need to know, prek–2* (pp. 46–66). Guilford Press.

Fisher, D., & Frey, N. (2018). Using questions to drive content area learning: Revising old favorites. *The Reading Teacher, 72*(3), 406–411.

Gardner, P. G. (2017). Discussing racial trauma using visual thinking strategies. *Language Arts, 94*(5), 338–345.

Housen, A., & Yenawine, P. (2002). *Visual thinking strategies curriculum.* Authors.

Joseph, L. M., Alber-Morgan, S., Cullen, J., & Rouse, C. (2015). The effects of self-questioning on comprehension: A literature review. *Reading & Writing Quarterly, 32*(2), 152–173.

Moeller, M., Cutler, K., Fiedler, D., & Weier, L. (2013). Visual thinking strategies = creative and critical thinking. *Phi Delta Kappan, 95*(3), 56–60.

National Council for the Social Studies. (2013). *The college, career, and civic life (C3) framework for social studies state standards: Guidance for enhancing the rigor of k–12 civics, economics, geography, and history.* Authors.

National Governors Association Center for Best Practices & Council of Chief State School Officers. (2010). *Common Core State Standards.* Authors.

Roberts, K. L., & Brugar, K. A. (2017). The view from here: Development of visual literacy in the social studies. *Reading Psychology, 38*(8), 733–777.

Roberts, K. L., & Brugar, K. A. (2014). Navigating maps to support comprehension: When textbooks don't have GPS. *The Geography Teacher, 11*(4), 149–163.

Roberts, K. L., Brugar, K. A., & Norman, R. N. (2014). Finding picture perfect graphical devices: An evaluation tool. *The Reading Teacher, 68*(4), 312–318.

Smolkowski, K., Stryker, L. A., Anderson, L., Marconi, P., & Abia-Smith, L. (2020). The visual thinking strategies approach to teaching argument writing: A professional development model. *The Elementary School Journal, 121*, 100–124.

Children's Literature and Lesson Resources Referenced

Burgoyne, J., Sayer, R., & Bennett., J. (1775). *A plan of the battle, on Bunkers Hill fought on the 17th of June*. London, printed for R. Sayer & J. Bennett. [Map]. Retrieved from the Library of Congress, https://www.loc.gov/item/gm71002452/.

Faden, W. (1776). *A plan of New York Island, with part of Long Island, Staten Island & East New Jersey, with a particular description of the engagement on the Woody Heights of Long Island.* https://militarymaps.rct.uk/american-war-of-independence-1775-83/long-island-new-york-and-staten-island-1776-a

Fawkes, J. (1776). *Battle of Long Island* [Painting]. https://www.britishbattles.com/war-of-the-revolution-1775-to-1783/battle-of-long-island/

Google. (2024). Google Earth Education. Google. https://google.com/earth/education/

Google. (n.d.). Google Geo Tools. Google. https://www.google.com/earth/education/

Leedy, L. (2003). *Mapping Penny's world*. Square Fish.

Library of Congress. (n.d.) Classroom materials at the Library of Congress. (n.d.). https://www.loc/gov/classroom-materials/

Library of Congress. (n.d.). Library of Congress: Finding primary source sets. Library of Congress. https://www.loc.gov/programs/teachersgetting-started-with-primary-sourcees/finding/

Library of Congress. (n.d.) Maps from the World Digital Library. Library of Congress. https://www.loc.gov/classroom-materials/maps-from-the-world-digital-library/

Library of Congress. (n.d.) *Teacher's guide: Analyzing maps*. Authors. https://www.loc.gov/static/programs/teachers/getting-started-with-primary-sources/documents/Analyzing_Maps.pdf

Library of Congress. (n.d.) Teacher's guides and analysis tool: Primary source analysis tool for students. Authors. https://www.loc.gov/programs/teachers/getting-started-with-primary-sources/guides/

Mount Vernon's Ladies Association. (2017). *New York campaign*. http://s3.amazonaws.com/mtv-main-assets/file/map/MntVernon_NYorkCampaign_26APR18.pdf

National Archives. (n.d.). National Archives analysis tools. National Archives. https://www.archives.gov/education/lessons/worksheets

National Geographic. (n.d.). National Geographic classroom map. National Geographic. https://education.nationalgeographic.org/resource/classroom-map/

Ritchie, S. (2009). *Follow that map! A first book of mapping skills*. Kids Can Press.

Xingmin07. (2012). *World topographic map* [digital image]. iStock. https://www.istockphoto.com/photo/world-topographic-map-gm182058785-20483752

Appendix A. *Teachers Guide: Analyzing Maps* (Library of Congress, n.d.).

TEACHER'S GUIDE
ANALYZING MAPS

Guide students with the sample questions as they respond to the primary source. Encourage them to go back and forth between the columns; there is no correct order.

OBSERVE

Have students identify and note details.

Sample Questions:

Describe what you see. · What do you notice first? · What size and shape is the map? · What graphical elements do you see? · What on the map looks strange or unfamiliar? · Describe anything that looks like it does not belong on a map. · What place or places does the map show? · What, if any, words do you see?

REFLECT

Encourage students to generate and test hypotheses about the source.

Why do you think this map was made? · Who do you think the audience was for this map? · How do you think this map was made? · How does it compare to current maps of this place? · What does this map tell you about what the people who made it knew and what they didn't? · If this map was made today, what would be different? · What would be the same?

QUESTION

Have students ask questions to lead to more observations and reflections.

What do you wonder about....

who? · what? · when? · where? · why? · how?

FURTHER INVESTIGATION

Help students to identify questions appropriate for further investigation, and to develop a research strategy for finding answers.

Sample Question: What more do you want to know, and how can you find out?

A few follow-up activity ideas:

Beginning
Have students write a brief description of the map in their own words.

Intermediate
Study three or more maps of a city or state at different time periods. Arrange them in chronological order. Discuss clues to the correct sequence.

Advanced
Search for maps of a city or state from different periods, then compile a list of changes over time and other differences and similarities between the maps.

For more tips on using primary sources, go to
http://www.loc.gov/teachers

CHAPTER 8

Engaging in Inquiry
PUTTING IT ALL TOGETHER

In previous chapters, we have explored skills and pedagogy related to individual, if overlapping, literacy constructs. In this chapter, we shift gears to provide examples of how the constructs of literacy can be used together to support full inquiries in K–2 and 3–5 classrooms. Instead of discussing particular skills and pedagogies, we share a bigger-picture view of what these skills and pedagogies might look like when used together to engage students in longer inquiries (perhaps spanning three to five lessons) and briefer inquiries (contained in one to two lessons).

What Is Inquiry?

Inquiry may not be a new idea to you, but maybe social studies inquiry isn't something you have seen or experienced. The idea of inquiry has been around for well over a century. John Dewey (1902) advocated for a form of inquiry-based instruction—application of knowledge and skills to real-world contexts—way back at the turn of the twentieth century.

In this century, you may have attended a professional-development session or learned a bit about the small-group inquiry model (Harvey & Daniels, 2009), guided inquiry (Kuhlthau et al., 2012), or even critical inquiry (Rodriguez & Swalwell, 2021). The ins and outs of each of these vary, and all of them could be (and are) the topics of whole books. However, the basic tenets of each are similar and reflected in the inquiry model included in this book, as well.

So, what exactly is inquiry? Most basically, inquiry is the act of asking and answering questions, typically with the goal of sharing the answers with an authentic audience or taking some sort of action. A key feature of inquiries is that questions posed can be answered in many different ways, depending on the person asking the questions, their perspectives or points of view, and the evidence or sources explored.

There is a wide variety of ways in which inquiry might be conducted in classrooms. Here, we give examples, knowing that inquiry occurs along a continuum of support, from teachers acting as guides through the whole inquiry to teachers coaching as students work more independently. Inquiry approaches also vary along other lines, often dependent upon the skills of students and time constraints (Swan et al., 2018). In a full inquiry, students' curiosities drive all stages (e.g., questions asked, source selection). However, in more abbreviated inquiries, the teacher may provide some aspects of the inquiry.

Because inquiry is not a skill, but rather the intersection of many skills, inquiry instruction is an approach to teaching that demands flexibility and responsiveness to your students, curricula, time, and context. Teachers cannot teach children to engage in all elements of inquiry within one inquiry experience. If, for example, the primary objectives of the inquiry are content learning and summarization, that's a lot to teach! As such, teachers might decide to provide the questions and sources. In contrast, if the objectives are content learning and asking open-ended questions, teachers might provide sources and structure the action steps or choose the audience.

Conducting inquiries as classroom practice often includes creating a series, scaffolded experiences in which learning of content and skills occurs in service of the inquiry. As students have experiences with necessary inquiry skills, such as generating new ideas, engaging in the writing process, linking evidence and claims, and participating in productive discussion (Brugar et al., 2024), they gain confidence and become increasingly independent. As students and teachers have experiences with inquiry, these instructional experiences may become more nuanced, with students' questions driving the inquiry while the teacher serves as a learner and a facilitator alongside the students.

INQUIRY IN THE SOCIAL STUDIES

When students engage in social studies inquiry, they are not collecting facts; rather, they are acting as citizens, economists, geographers, and historians. Students are asking questions that are both rooted in those disciplines as well as of interest to the larger community beyond that discipline. For example, students might ask, "Why does our community have sidewalks on only one side of the street?" This is a question that has civic, economic, geographic, and historic facets. Further, the answers or conclusions students draw have academic and social implications.

As students move through an inquiry, generally, they "build knowledge that is deep and lasting, because their learning connects to their curiosities and interests—and because it has a real-world purpose: they use it to inform others, improve their community, or help set goals for the future" (InquirED, 2023).

To facilitate inquiry, the National Council for the Social Studies (2013) frames inquiry as an arc (Table 8.1). All inquiries begin with a compelling question, often (but not always) developed by students. Students then apply disciplinary lenses of civics, economics, geography, and history as they develop and address supporting questions. They then use these lenses as they evaluate and use sources to answer the supporting and, ultimately, the compelling questions. As a final step, and lending to the authenticity of inquiry, students communicate what they have learned with an audience or take some sort of action rooted in their learning.

Table 8.1. Dimensions of the C3 Framework Inquiry Arc

Dimension	Explanation
Dimension 1: Developing questions and planning inquiries	Developing questions to investigate societal issues, trends, and events is an integral part of the inquiry process. The National Council for the Social Studies (NCSS) describes two types of questions: compelling and supporting. Compelling questions are those that focus on larger curiosities, reflecting a social concern and enduring issue in one or more social studies disciplines (e.g., civics, economics, geography, history), concepts, issues, or ideas. Supporting questions are designed to provide concrete scaffolding. Answering supporting questions helps students compile information that will be helpful to address the compelling question.
Dimension 2: Applying disciplinary tools and concepts (in the areas of civics, economics, geography, and history)	The NCSS describes the application of disciplinary concepts and tools as the "backbone for the Inquiry Arc" (2013, p. 17). As part of this dimension, students utilize prior knowledge as well as newly acquired understandings of social studies concepts and tools as they develop and refine their questions and pursue their inquiry.
Dimension 3: Evaluating sources and using evidence	Students work toward reaching conclusions about societal issues, trends, and events by collecting evidence and evaluating its usefulness in developing causal explanations.
Dimension 4: Communicating conclusions and taking informed action	Students demonstrate content and conceptual understandings through a thoughtful reflection of the inquiry process.

Source: National Council for the Social Studies, 2013.

Why Is Inquiry Important?

Inquiry is a dynamic practice that links students to the world beyond school through their interests and curiosities. Yet, social studies inquiry does not always happen at the elementary level. Likely, this is in part due to three decades of marginalization of social studies in elementary classrooms (e.g., Fitchett & Haefner, 2010; Houser, 1995). However, if you've made it this far in the book, you're almost certainly planning to teach social studies, and inquiry is an ideal way to address multiple social studies standards and the literacy skills that provide access to them.

If we start from the premise that social studies is important (and we are firmly in that camp), then inquiry in the social studies is also important. As you might recall from Chapter 1, an important goal of social studies is preparing students to be engaged citizens—critical thinkers who are prepared to examine the past, participate in the present, and shape the future. Yes, teachers are responsible for teaching particular things in each grade, but, more importantly, teachers prepare students to go out in the world and (pardon the cliché) become lifelong learners, wonderers, and citizens.

Inquiry situates students as active and integral actors in their own learning. Students can become better askers of questions, authentic questions that will carry them beyond the classroom and prepare them to ask authentic questions in their communities and world. Students who engage in inquiry-based practice negotiate various forms of evidence, preparing them to do so in their future when, for example, they may hear about an issue and seek sources to learn more about it before developing an opinion or taking an action on the issue.

Pedagogies for Inquiry

In our previous chapters we have shared particular pedagogies; this chapter will be a bit different. Conducting an inquiry involves a wide collection of skills and pedagogies. So, for example, an inquiry might include teachers engaging students in conversation, but the pedagogy for structuring the conversation is a decision best made by the teacher, who is better positioned to make instructional decisions based on students' skills, knowledge, and previous experiences (Thacker et al., 2018).

In general, but particularly in the elementary grades, inquiries are scaffolded learning experiences. Inquiry simultaneously provides opportunities for students to demonstrate the skills they have learned (or are learning) and for teachers to scaffold. Modeling, having shared interactions, coaching students who are working independently and in groups, and providing opportunities for independent work are all valuable pedagogical choices over the course of an inquiry. Importantly, the level of scaffolding provided can vary both by student and by stage of the inquiry, based on teachers' professional knowledge.

Throughout this book, you have read about the possibilities of and opportunities for rich social studies teaching and learning through the use of reading, writing, speaking, listening, viewing, and creating. All these things can't be instructional foci at the same time. Understanding the role of scaffolding in inquiry is important. Inquiry requires the use of many skill sets that are learned as students engage in the inquiry process.

This means that, sometimes, students need to use skills they don't possess or are not yet proficient in. That's OK. Teachers stand in the gap, providing just enough support for students to be able to take on the task. Teachers also teach inquiry skills (of course), but not everything! While inquiry is a great place for instruction because students are generally quite motivated to learn, as in any other lesson, one or two teaching points are plenty.

All this is said as a simple reminder to exercise professional judgment as you engage in inquiry with your students. Students may need you to facilitate or guide the activities associated with a supporting question or may be ready to independently talk about the discussion question posed that stages the inquiry. You know your students best and your judgment of their capabilities and needs is invaluable for a successful inquiry.

INQUIRY DESIGN MODEL BLUEPRINTS AND FOCUSED INQUIRIES

For the two classroom applications in this chapter, we will model the use of the Inquiry Design Model (IDM) (Swan et al., 2013, 2022; Appendix A) and an abbreviated version of the IDM, Focused Inquiry (Swan et al., 2018; Appendix B). Both are designed to organize inquiries in ways that are succinct and manageable in classrooms, providing both structure and flexibility for teachers. Inherent in these models is the expectation of knowledge and expertise of teachers about their content area, students' needs and abilities, and their context.

Our choice to use the focused inquiry for the K–2 example and the full inquiry for the 3–5 example should not be interpreted to mean that the different formats are more or less appropriate for the different grade levels. The decision of which format to use hinges on several variables, and chief among them is how much time is available for the inquiry.

Many fully-prepared IDMs on a variety of topics are available at each grade level can be found at C3 Teachers, Inquiries Archives (https://c3teachers.org/inquiries/). These examples are not meant to be all-inclusive, scripted lessons. Rather, they are meant to be well-formed outlines, inclusive of the resources needed to implement them, but also with room for teachers to modify the inquiries as appropriate for their context.

The IDM aligns well with the premise of this book and the ways in which we navigate elementary-school teaching and learning. Grant, Lee, and Swan state, "IDM is a distinctive approach to creating curriculum and instructional materials that honors teachers' knowledge and expertise, avoids over-prescription, and focuses on the central elements of the instructional design process as envisioned in the Inquiry Arc of the *College, Career, and Civic Life (C3) Framework for State Social Studies Standards* (National Council for the Social Studies, 2013)" (2015, p. 123).

Having established this foundational understanding of inquiry, we can now address how both the IDM blueprint and focused inquiries include several key elements. Each begins with a compelling question and a notation of the standards addressed. According to Swan and colleagues, compelling questions are "intellectually meaty" and "student-friendly." This means questions address an issue or a concern across a variety of social science disciplines and align with students' interests and abilities.

So that educators may lead students to address the compelling question of an inquiry, the model walks educators through several more categories of information. The "Staging the Inquiry" section provides the "hook" or introduction to the inquiry, framing the content to be explored, skills to be used, or both. Next are the supporting questions. Supporting questions tend to be more concrete than compelling questions, and they help students identify concrete information or understandings to move them toward being able to answer the compelling question. Typically, there are three to four supporting questions in a full IDM and one in a focused inquiry, each aligned with a formative assessment.

The models also include a series of featured sources that align with each supporting question and corresponding formative assessment. These featured sources may be historic or contemporary and may be multimodal: audio, visual, or text sources. Whether you're using a published IDM or focused inquiry or creating your own model, getting all of these sources into one easily accessible place makes inquiries run much more smoothly!

Finally, both the IDM blueprint and focused inquiry conclude with a summative assessment and "taking action" tasks. The summative assessment measures students' cumulative understandings, which were built during the inquiry, as well as their abilities to respond to the compelling question. When students take action, they are en-

Focused Inquiry
Suggested Grade Levels: K–2

	Compelling Question
	Where does our food come from?
C3 Framework Indicator	D2.Eco.4.K–2. Describe the goods and services that people in the local community produce and those that are produced in other communities.
***Common Core State Standards* (English Language Arts)**	W.K.8: With guidance and support from adults, recall information from experiences or gather information from provided sources to answer a question. W.1.8: With guidance and support from adults, recall information from experiences or gather information from provided sources to answer a question. W.2.8: Recall information from experiences or gather information from provided sources to answer a question.
Staging the Question	Read the book *How to Make an Apple Pie and See the World*, by Marjorie Priceman (1994). Use the world map that is part of the endpapers to point out the countries as the main character gathers ingredients. As you read, ask students to make predictions about which ingredients she might find in each country.

Supporting Question
What food can we produce in our state?

Formative Performance Task
Create a T-chart documenting foods that can and cannot be grown in your state.

Featured Sources
Michigan Agricultural Facts and Figures (Michigan Department of Agriculture & Rural Development, n.d.)
Growing and Harvesting in Michigan (Urban Farmer, 2018)
Students' lived experiences!

Summative Performance Task	**Argument**
Each student creates one page of a class book of foods that can and cannot be grown in your state, citing evidence to back the claim.	Choose an agricultural product and make a claim about whether it does or does not grow in your state.
	Extensions
	Create a map showing where various agricultural products are produced in your state. Investigate ingredients that are not produced in your state to determine where they are produced.

Figure 8.1. Focused Inquiry, Suggested Grade Levels: K-2.

couraged to share what they have learned with a wider audience. This may be sharing inquiry findings with students in another class or speaking to the city council about an important issue; for example, in the upper elementary scenario, students are encouraged to speak to their school boards about school lunches.

CLASSROOM APPLICATIONS, K–2

In this lesson, we use the focused inquiry template (Swan et al., 2018). The template includes many of the same elements as are in our other lesson examples, but these elements are formatted in a different way. A blank template is included at the end of this chapter. Below, we first share a completed template designed for first-grade learners. Then, following the completed template, we walk through each section, describing what is included and our thought processes as we designed the inquiry.

Because K–2 social studies content is focused more locally than nationally or globally, this inquiry is based on what can be grown or produced in students' states and what must be grown elsewhere. The state used in this example is Michigan, and, accordingly, some of the featured sources are also Michigan specific. However, similar reputable resources exist for other states and can generally be located by a quick Google search and vetting of the organizations and publishers. To help you identify similar sources appropriate to your state, we have provided brief descriptions of each in the "Featured Resources" section.

STAGING THE INQUIRY

Start the inquiry with a whole-group reading of the book *How to Make an Apple Pie and See the World*, by Marjorie Priceman (1994). Before starting the book, let students know that, today, they're going to think about where their food comes from. Tell them that, in the story, the main character is going to make an apple pie, but first, she has to gather her ingredients—the different foods that are part of her pie recipe. As you read, pose questions to the students such as the following:

- The store is closed! How do you think she can get the ingredients for her pie now?
- Oh! She's headed to Italy! Let's look back at the list of ingredients on the first page. What do you think she will be looking for in Italy?
- Why would she go to France to find a chicken? There is no chicken in apple pie!

The list of ingredients on the first page of the story is a great reference for what goes into the pie as students are thinking about which ingredient might come from each place.

[After reading, facilitate a discussion with students about what they learned about where different foods might come from. Remind students that, in this story, the main character had to travel to all those places to get ingredients for a pie, which we probably wouldn't do.] *"But what can the story help us understand about where food comes from before we find it in grocery stores?"*

SUPPORTING QUESTION

The supporting question for this inquiry, *What food can we produce in our state?*, moves students from thinking about all the places ingredients might come from to what ingredients might be produced or grown in their own state. Students will prepare to answer this question by creating a list of foods and classifying them by where they grow in the performance task. Resources to verify classification include publications by the State Department of Agriculture and the Urban Farmer organization as well as students' own lived experiences.

FORMATIVE PERFORMANCE TASK

In the formative performance task, students begin by listing ingredients that they like to eat or use. Explain to students that ingredients are types of foods that can be used in recipes but that can also be eaten on their own. You may note, for example, that cherries and potatoes are ingredients because they can be eaten on their own or used as part of a recipe. You may explain that pie, however, is not an ingredient because you would need to combine many ingredients to make it.

As students brainstorm ideas of ingredients, you can either put them all in one list or put each on a sticky note or index card. Once students have provided all of their ideas, shift the conversation to whether the ingredients can be produced in their state. Depending on students' skill levels, they can either work in small groups to explore the featured sources or explore the resources as a whole class.

If students work in small groups, each group should be assigned about the same number of ingredients to investigate. If you chose to record the ingredients on sticky notes or index cards, those can be given to the students as they work. Students will browse the *Michigan Agricultural Facts and Figures* source and the "What to Plant and When" section of the *Growing and Harvesting in Michigan* source (substituting state-appropriate sources, as needed), looking for evidence that the ingredient can be produced in their state. They can also use their own experiences, for example, having grown it in their garden or having seen the ingredient on a local farm.

If students are not able to locate evidence in any source indicating that the ingredient can be produced in their state, they will set it aside for future investigation. To find more information, students might do an internet search or ask a grocery store staff member.

FEATURED SOURCES

Please note that, for web-based resources, we have provided the URL. However, in most cases, it is much more efficient just to do a Google search of the title of the document. Also, these resources are state specific due to the nature of the inquiry questions. Similar resources are available for other states. Good starting places include your state department of agriculture or farm council.

Figure 8.2. *Michigan Agricultural Facts & Figures* (Michigan Department of Agriculture & Rural Development, n.d.).

Text Summary: This source provides interesting facts and figures about crops and other agricultural produces (e.g., milk, beef) that are produced in Michigan. Similar sources are available for many other states.

Students have spent a great deal of time in their own communities and may have firsthand experiences that help them answer the question of whether ingredients can be produced in the state. For example, one student may raise chickens and know that eggs can be produced in the state. Another may have visited an urban community garden and seen various fruits and vegetables growing. These are important experiences and also valuable forms of evidence!

SUMMATIVE PERFORMANCE TASK

For the summative performance task, students will each create one page of a class book. Each page will include an illustration or photograph and describe an ingredient and where it is produced (their state or elsewhere). The image and text will answer the compelling question, *Where does our food come from?* This book may be shared with other classes, in the school library, or used as a resource for a thematic unit.

Resources for Inquiry: K–2

Alternative Sources for This Inquiry

Brittanica Kids (Encyclopedia Brittanica, 2024): This online encyclopedia contains entries for each state, with sections on agriculture, fishing, and forestry. https://kids.britannica.com/

The *Everybody* Series (Dooley, various years): This series of narrative picture books discusses foods that are common across cultures (i.e., rice, noodles, bread, soup) and the different ways they are prepared, including recipes!

Finding Stuff Out—"Where Does Food Come From?" Season 4, Episode 2 (9 Story Fun): This video runs for twenty-one and a half minutes and addresses the question, "Where would we get food from if there were no grocery stores?" https://www.youtube.com/watch?v=Qfm5ExOwI0w

Teacher Resources for Inquiry

"Questions, Tasks, Sources: Focusing on the Essence of Inquiry" (Swan et al., 2018): This short article provides an overview of focused inquiries and describes, in detail, each component. https://www.socialstudies.org/system/files/publications/articles/se_8203133_1.pdf

Revolution of Ideas: A Decade of C3 Inquiry (Swan et al., 2023): This book contains a collection of twenty-seven articles about how the *C3 Framework* is integrated into standards, curriculum, instruction, and assessment.

CLASSROOM APPLICATIONS, 3–5

For our later elementary example, we use the IDM blueprint (Swan et al., 2013). (A blank template is included at the end of this chapter.) Below, you will read a completed template designed for third-grade learners. You may notice there are fewer details than in some publicly available lesson plans you come across. This provides a framework and ideas for you to adapt for your students and the learning context. Then, following the completed template, we describe each section, sharing what we included and our thought processes as we designed this inquiry.

	Inquiry Design Model Blueprint™ **Suggested Grade Levels: 3–5**
Compelling Question	Why do we eat what we eat?
C3 Framework Indicators	D2.Eco.4.3–5. Explain why individuals and businesses specialize and trade.
	D2.Eco.1.3–5. Compare the benefits and costs of individual choices.
	D2.Eco.2.3–5. Identify positive and negative incentives that influence the decisions people make.
Common Core State Standards (English Language Arts)	RI.3.7. Use information gained from illustrations (e.g., maps, photographs) and the words in a text to demonstrate understanding of the text (e.g., where, when, why, and how key events occur).
	RI.4.7 Interpret information presented visually, orally, or quantitatively (e.g., in charts, graphs, diagrams, timelines, animations, or interactive elements on Web pages), and explain how the information contributes to an understanding of the text in which it appears.
	RI.5.7 Draw on information from multiple print or digital sources, demonstrating the ability to locate an answer to a question quickly or to solve a problem efficiently.
	W.3.2. Write informative/explanatory texts to examine a topic and convey ideas and information clearly.
	W.4.2. Write informative/explanatory texts to examine a topic and convey ideas and information clearly.
	W.5.2. Write informative/explanatory texts to examine a topic and convey ideas and information clearly.
Staging the Inquiry	Read aloud *Try It! How Frieda Caplan Changed the Way We Eat* (Rockcliff, 2021), a book about a woman who imported many different fruits and vegetables that we enjoy eating into the United States. Ask students to record the fruits and vegetables Caplan imported and where she imported them from.

Figure 8.3. Inquiry Design Model Blueprint™, Suggested Grade Levels: 3-5.

Supporting Question 1	Supporting Question 2	Supporting Question 3
Where does our school lunch come from?	If we ate only locally, what would we eat for lunch?	What are the implications of our food choices?
Formative Performance Task	**Formative Performance Task**	**Formative Performance Task**
Complete a 3-2-1 to answer supporting question 1.	Create an infographic identifying and explaining local foods.	Complete a benefits and costs graphic organizer.
Featured Sources	**Featured Sources**	**Featured Sources**
State Archives about School Lunches, e.g., Oklahoma School Lunch Newsletter, 1954 (https://digitalprairie.ok.gov/digital/collection/okresources/id/92930). United States Department of Agriculture, Food and Nutrition Services, School Lunch https://www.fns.usda.gov/tn/school-lunch-resources Your school breakfast and/or lunch menus	*Mapped: Where Does Our Food Come From?* https://www.visualcapitalist.com/sp/where-does-our-food-come-from/	United States Department of Agriculture, Food Security and Access https://www.nutrition.gov/topics/food-security-and-access

Summative Performance Task	**Argument** What foods should be included in school lunches and/or breakfasts? Why are those foods important? Students may consider nutrition, access, environmental impact, cost, kid-friendliness, interest, etc.
	Extension Explore the accessibility of food in your local community.
Taking Informed Action	**Understand:** Browse school meal menus from schools throughout your school district (from other elementary schools, middle schools, and high schools). Notice there may be different food items available at various school sites. **Assess:** Make note of the differences and consider why those differences might be. **Act:** Design a school meal menu that meets the needs of your local community and propose it to the school board.

Figure 8.3. (Continued)

STAGING THE INQUIRY

Begin this inquiry with a read aloud of *Try It!: How Frieda Caplan Changed the Way We Eat* (Rockliff, 2021). (If you don't have a copy of the book, there are excellent read alouds of it available on YouTube.) Before you read, ask your students, "Have you ever thought about where the food you eat comes from?" Students may share answers like "the grocery store" or "a farm." Share with students that they will be learning about a woman who imported many different fruits and vegetables that we enjoy eating into the United States. Introduce or remind students that to "import" means to bring into one country from another.

As you read, ask students to record the fruits and vegetables that Caplan imported and where she imported them from. This information could be recorded on a T-chart or another similar graphic organizer that the class completes together. After reading, review the fruits and vegetables identified in the text (possible taste tests!?!). Ask students to consider the benefits and costs of having these foods available to them. For example, students may really enjoy eating kiwis—that's a benefit. A cost might be money spent on fuel to import kiwis or transport them across the country to places where kiwis cannot grow.

> ## Recommended Text
>
> *Try It!* is a biography of the produce pioneer, Frieda Caplan, who was known as the "Mushroom Queen." In 1956, Caplan started working at the Seventh Street Produce Market in Los Angeles, where she saw lots of apples, potatoes, and tomatoes. Caplan saw an opportunity to bring different fruits and vegetables into Americans' homes. She imported mushrooms, snap peas, kiwis, seedless watermelons, and mangos.

SUPPORTING QUESTION 1

For supporting question 1, *Where does our school lunch come from?*, students will engage in an authentic investigation of their school cafeteria. To begin, share a primary source that is associated with school lunches, for example, the *School Lunch, Supper Menus Saturday, February 28, 1959* from the Star Tribune Archives (Figure 8.4).

Next, you can either share the school lunch menus or ask students to gather the lunch menus. Ask students to discuss the similarities and differences between the offerings on this 1959 menu and what is offered as part of their school meals. Ask them, "What are the similarities (if any)?"; "What are the differences?"; and "Further, why might there be differences?"

Ask students to identify the various food items and possible ingredients in their school lunch menus and to create a list. With that list, plan a visit to the cafeteria and have a conversation with cafeteria personnel about the food items on the menu. Students may ask, "Who selected these items?"; "Where does the food come from?"; "What is your favorite thing to make?"; "What is your favorite thing to serve?"; and "What is your favorite thing to eat from the menu?" Following this visit, ask students to complete a "3-2-1" to answer supporting question 1. Students will note three things they learned about school lunch items in the past and present, two things they are wondering about foods in schools, and one thing they enjoyed learning.

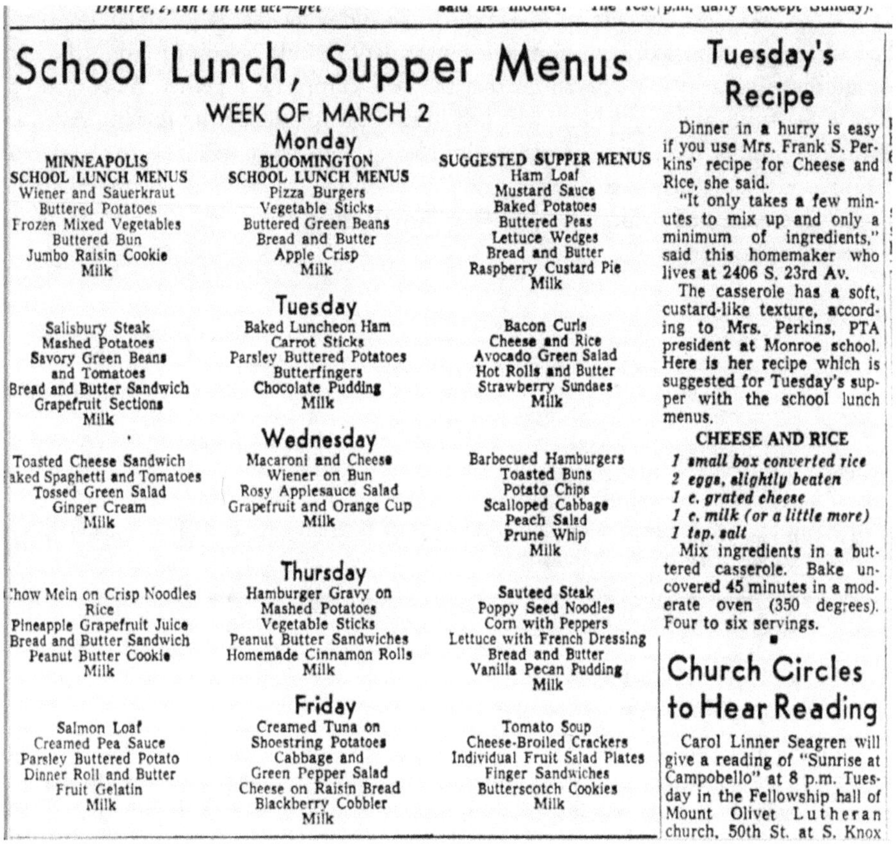

School Lunch, Supper Menus
WEEK OF MARCH 2
Monday

MINNEAPOLIS SCHOOL LUNCH MENUS
Wiener and Sauerkraut
Buttered Potatoes
Frozen Mixed Vegetables
Buttered Bun
Jumbo Raisin Cookie
Milk

BLOOMINGTON SCHOOL LUNCH MENUS
Pizza Burgers
Vegetable Sticks
Buttered Green Beans
Bread and Butter
Apple Crisp
Milk

SUGGESTED SUPPER MENUS
Ham Loaf
Mustard Sauce
Baked Potatoes
Buttered Peas
Lettuce Wedges
Bread and Butter
Raspberry Custard Pie
Milk

Tuesday

Salisbury Steak
Mashed Potatoes
Savory Green Beans and Tomatoes
Bread and Butter Sandwich
Grapefruit Sections
Milk

Baked Luncheon Ham
Carrot Sticks
Parsley Buttered Potatoes
Butterfingers
Chocolate Pudding
Milk

Bacon Curls
Cheese and Rice
Avocado Green Salad
Hot Rolls and Butter
Strawberry Sundaes
Milk

Wednesday

Toasted Cheese Sandwich
Baked Spaghetti and Tomatoes
Tossed Green Salad
Ginger Cream
Milk

Macaroni and Cheese
Wiener on Bun
Rosy Applesauce Salad
Grapefruit and Orange Cup
Milk

Barbecued Hamburgers
Toasted Buns
Potato Chips
Scalloped Cabbage
Peach Salad
Prune Whip
Milk

Thursday

Chow Mein on Crisp Noodles
Rice
Pineapple Grapefruit Juice
Bread and Butter Sandwich
Peanut Butter Cookie
Milk

Hamburger Gravy on Mashed Potatoes
Vegetable Sticks
Peanut Butter Sandwiches
Homemade Cinnamon Rolls
Milk

Sauteed Steak
Poppy Seed Noodles
Corn with Peppers
Lettuce with French Dressing
Bread and Butter
Vanilla Pecan Pudding
Milk

Friday

Salmon Loaf
Creamed Pea Sauce
Parsley Buttered Potato
Dinner Roll and Butter
Fruit Gelatin
Milk

Creamed Tuna on Shoestring Potatoes
Cabbage and Green Pepper Salad
Cheese on Raisin Bread
Blackberry Cobbler
Milk

Tomato Soup
Cheese-Broiled Crackers
Individual Fruit Salad Plates
Finger Sandwiches
Butterscotch Cookies
Milk

Tuesday's Recipe

Dinner in a hurry is easy if you use Mrs. Frank S. Perkins' recipe for Cheese and Rice, she said.

"It only takes a few minutes to mix up and only a minimum of ingredients," said this homemaker who lives at 2406 S. 23rd Av.

The casserole has a soft, custard-like texture, according to Mrs. Perkins, PTA president at Monroe school. Here is her recipe which is suggested for Tuesday's supper with the school lunch menus.

CHEESE AND RICE
1 small box converted rice
2 eggs, slightly beaten
1 c. grated cheese
1 c. milk (or a little more)
1 tsp. salt

Mix ingredients in a buttered casserole. Bake uncovered 45 minutes in a moderate oven (350 degrees). Four to six servings.

Church Circles to Hear Reading

Carol Linner Seagren will give a reading of "Sunrise at Campobello" at 8 p.m. Tuesday in the Fellowship hall of Mount Olivet Lutheran church, 50th St. at S. Knox

Figure 8.4. "School Lunch, Supper Menus Saturday," February 28, 1959, from the *Star Tribune Archives*.

SUPPORTING QUESTION 2

Today, the United States produces and has access to lots of different foods. That has not always been the case. To help students think about and understand foods that are locally produced, share *Where Does Our Food Come From?* (https://www.visual-capitalist.com/sp/where-does-our-food-come-from/). Consider using visual thinking strategies (VTS, Housen & Yenawine, 2002) in which students will analyze the map to share observations, make assertations with evidence, and ask questions about what they view. (See Chapter 7 for additional information on VTS.)

Next, students will transition to supporting question 2, *If we only ate locally today, what would we eat for lunch?* Using maps and other data that show foods grown or produced in your local community (a Google search of your particular location should provide a variety of options), task students with creating an infographic to answer supporting question 2. Remember, an infographic is a visual representation of data. For additional support to create infographics, go to Adobe (https://www.adobe.com/uk/express/learn/blog/what-is-an-infographic) or Canva (https://www.canva.com/learn/how-to-make-an-infographic/).

SUPPORTING QUESTION 3

Supporting question 3, *What are the implications of our food choices?*, has students explore the economic concept of opportunity costs. Introduce students to or remind students of the definition of opportunity costs (i.e., those things being given up or sacrificed when a decision is made). For example, if I am deciding how to use my free time during the weekend and I choose to read a book rather than ride my bike, the opportunity cost is time not riding my bike.

Ask students to create their dream menus for a day, identifying what would they eat for breakfast, lunch, and dinner (Figure 8.5 and Appendix C). Based on those dream menus, they will consider the benefits and costs of their food choices. For example, if a student identifies a WhatABurger burger and fries (see "Map 26", https://www.vox.com/a/explain-food-america) for dinner and lives in Michigan, the student could note a benefit being "tastes good, kid-friendly" and the costs being "time and expense because the closest WhatABurger is one thousand miles away in Texas."

SUMMATIVE PERFORMANCE TASK

After completing investigations associated with supporting questions 1, 2, and 3, students will present a claim with evidence to answer the questions: *What foods should be included in school lunches/breakfasts? Why are those foods important?* In order to support their claims, students should include consideration of and evidence associated with the costs and benefits of their choices. For example, they may reference the accessibility of particular foods, nutritional value, expense, environmental impact, and kid-friendliness.

Food Item	Ingredients	Benefits (e.g., nutritional, economical, environmental, time-related)	Costs (e.g., nutritional, economical, environmental, time-related)
Breakfast			
Lunch			
Dinner			

Figure 8.5. Benefits and Costs Graphic Organizer.

To extend students' arguments, individuals, small groups, or the whole class may explore the accessibility of food within their community. This could involve guest speakers from a local food pantry, grocery store, or farm bureau.

Resources for Inquiry: 3-5

Alternative Student Sources for this Inquiry

Ultimate Food Atlas: Maps, Games, Recipes, and More for Hours of Delicious Fun (Castalado & Mihaly, 2022): This informational text presents a wide variety of things associated with food around the world.

What the World Eats (D'Auision & Menzel, 2008): Through photographs and text, this book describes what people eat around the world.

The World That Feeds Us (Castalado, 2023): This informational text describes aspects of farming, from crops to seasonality to pesticides.

"What School Lunch Looked Like Each Decade Since 1900" (Wells, 2021): This article presents pictures of school lunches. https://www.mentalfloss.com/article/87238/what-school-lunch-looked-each-decade-past-century

United States Department of Agriculture, Food Access Resource Atlas: This online resource contains entries for each state associated with food access. https://www.ers.usda.gov/data-products/food-access-research-atlas/

Forty Maps That Explain Food in America (Klein & Locke, 2014): This online collection of maps and other data visualizations describe a variety of issues about food, particularly accessibility. https://www.vox.com/a/explain-food-america

Teacher Resources for Inquiry

Inquiry-Based Practice in Social Studies Education (Grant, Swan, & Lee, 2022): This book introduces inquiry-based practices in social studies classrooms and encourages readers to engage in these practices to transform their classrooms.

Real Classrooms, Real Teachers: The C3 Inquiry in Practice (Brugar & Roberts, 2021): The C3 framework serves as a foundation for this book, which provides examples of and ideas for working with elementary and middle school students to build social studies skills and knowledge in order to become independent learners and thinkers.

Wrapping Up

There are lots of ways to teach social studies. Approaching social studies through inquiry-based practices creates spaces for students to authentically explore questions and topics they are curious about, using the multimodal literacy and interdisciplinary skills they have while building new skills. The opportunities for students to inquire model their current and future involvement as citizens in communities. Being an engaged citizen is a practiced skill. It doesn't happen because something happened one time; rather, citizenship is exercised consistently and over time (kind of like training for a marathon).

Chat and Change

"Chat and change" topics can be used as a menu of discussion starters for professional learning communities (PLCs), teacher education courses, or book clubs. You can also use them to guide your individual thinking about how to move the instructional practices in the chapter into your classroom.

- What elements of inquiry are you and your students already familiar with? What practices would be new for you? For your students?
- In considering your time constraints and comfort level, would an IDM blueprint or focused inquiry be a better fit for your students? Why?
- What questions are you interested in exploring with your students?
- How might you go about identifying a variety of sources that are content specific, age and skill appropriate, and interesting to your students?
- After reading this chapter or book, what is your step one? What is one thing you can do to move your teaching practice forward to support the skills students need to actively engage in social studies learning and/or inquiry?

References

Brugar, K. A., & Roberts, K. L. (Eds.). (2021). *Real classrooms, real teachers: The C3 inquiry in practice.* Information Age Publishing.

Brugar, K. A., Roberts, K. L., & Cuenca, A. (2024). Inquiry on inquiry: Examining student actions required in elementary Inquiry Design Models. *Journal of Social Studies, 48*(2), 102–113.

C3 Teachers. (2021). Inquiries. https://c3teachers.org/inquiries

Grant, S. G., Swan, K., & Lee, J. (2022). *Inquiry-based practice in social studies education* (2nd ed.). Routledge.

Harvey, S., & Harvey, D. (2009). *Comprehension & collaboration: Inquiry circles in action.* Heinemann.

Houser, N. (1995). Social studies on the back burner: Views from the field. *Theory and Research in Social Education, 23*(2), 147–168.

Kuhlthau, C. C., Maniotes, L. K., & Caspari, A. K. (2012). *Guided inquiry design: A framework for inquiry in your school.* Libraries Unlimited Guided Inquiry.

Michigan Department of Agriculture & Rural Development. (n.d.). *Michigan agricultural facts and figures.* Michigan.gov. https://www.michigan.gov/-/media/Project/Websites/mdard/documents/business-development/mi_ag_facts_figures.pdf?rev=880dd023f529407cb2580b90503d7d7d

National Council for the Social Studies. (2013). *The college, career, and civic life (C3) framework for social studies state standards: Guidance for enhancing the rigor of K–12 civics, economics, geography, and history.* NCSS.

Rodriguez, N., & Swalwell, K. (2021). *Social studies for a better world.* Norton Books.

Swan, K., Grant, S. G., & Lee, J. (2023). *Revolution of ideas: A decade of C3 inquiry.* National Council for the Social Studies.

Swan, K., Lee, J., & Grant, S. G. (2018). Questions, tasks, and sources: Focusing on the essence of inquiry. *Social Education, 82*(3), 133–137.

Thacker, E. S., Friedman, A. M., Fitchett, P. G., Journell, W., & Lee, J. K. (2018). Exploring how an elementary teacher plans and implements social studies inquiry. *The Social Studies*, *109*(2), 85–100. https://doi.org/10.1080/00377996.2018.1451983

Urban Farmer. (2018). *Growing and harvesting in Michigan*. Urban Farmer. https://www.uf-seeds.com/on/demandware.static/-/Sites-UrbanFarmer-Library/default/dw23121e3a/images/content/Michigan.pdf

Children's Literature and Lesson Resources Referenced

9 Story Fun. (2018, August 30). *Finding stuff out: "Where does food come from?,"* season 4, episode 2 [Video]. https://www.youtube.com/watch?v=Qfm5ExOwI0w

Encyclopedia Brittanica. (2024). *Brittanica Kids*. https://kids.britannica.com/

Castaldo, N. (2023). *The world that feeds us*. Quarto Publishing plc.

Castaldo, N., & Mihaly, C. (2022). *Ultimate food atlas: Maps, games, recipes, and more for hours of delicious fun*. National Geographic Kids.

D'Aluisio, F., & Menzel, P. (2008). *What the world eats*. Tricycle Press.

Klein, E., & Locke, S. (2014, June 9). *Forty maps that explain food in America*. Vox. https://www.vox.com/a/explain-food-america

Priceman, M. (1994). *How to make an apple pie and see the world*. Dragonfly Books.

Rockliff, M. (2021). *Try it!: How Frieda Caplan changed the way we eat*. Beach Lane Books.

Rotner, S. (2006). *Where does food come from?* Millbrook Press.

Star Tribune Archive. (2024). *Lunch and supper menus, 1959*. https://www.newspapers.com/paper/star-tribune/4474/

United States Department of Agriculture. (2024, April 17). *Food access resource atlas*. https://www.ers.usda.gov/data-products/food-access-research-atlas/

Wells, J. (2021, August 3). *What school lunch looked like each decade since 1900*. Mental Floss. https://www.mentalfloss.com/article/87238/what-school-lunch-looked-each-decade-past-century

Appendix A. Inquiry Design Model (IDM) Blueprint™ Template (Swan et al., 2013, 2022)

Inquiry Design Model (IDM) Blueprint™ Suggested Grade Level(s):			
Compelling Question			
C3 Framework Common Core State Standards (English Language Arts)			
Staging the Inquiry			
Supporting Question 1		**Supporting Question 2**	**Supporting Question 3**
Formative Performance Task		**Formative Performance Task**	**Formative Performance Task**
Featured Sources		**Featured Sources**	**Featured Sources**
Summative Performance Task	Argument		
	Extension		
Taking Informed Action	Understand: Assess: Act:		

Source: Swan et al., 2013, 2022.

Appendix B. Focused Inquiry Template (Swan et al., 2018)

Focused Inquiry **Suggested Grade Level(s):**	
Compelling Question	
C3 Framework Indicator **Common Core State Standards (English Language Arts)**	
Staging the Question	
Supporting Question	
Formative Performance Task	
Featured Sources	
Summative Performance Task	**Argument:**
	Extension:

Source: Swan et al., 2018.

Appendix C. Benefits and Costs Graphic Organizer

Food Item	Ingredients	**Benefits** (e.g., nutritional, economical, environmental, time-related)	**Costs** (e.g., nutritional, economical, environmental, time-related)
Breakfast			
Lunch			
Dinner			

CHAPTER 9

Final Thoughts

We have arrived at the end of the book. Thank you for joining us on this journey through some of our favorite topics. While we have you for just a few more minutes, we'll keep it short and sweet and share some key takeaways and ideas for where you might go to continue your exploration of social studies, literacy, and inquiry.

Ten Teachable Takeaways

- Teaching social studies is important—it is the understanding of the world we live in, past, present, and future. Kids need social studies.
- Students' voices and experiences in social studies are the foundations for their involvement and engagement as citizens in communities, so they need opportunities and invitations to make their voices heard!
- Teaching social studies requires that we teach not only content and skills but also the skills students need to learn content with increasing independence.
- Teachers are learners of social studies skills and knowledge as well as pedagogy! The world is changing every day, and we need to be aware of changes, new ideas, and understandings associated with civics, economics, geography, history, and how we teach them.
- Teachers teach students and are responsible for teaching standards. There are lots of engaging and effective ways to do that and nearly endless source materials. Use your professional knowledge, and teach in the ways that best support and engage your learners.
- Inquiry allows students and teachers to be curious learners.
- Reading and writing aren't enough. Social studies sources and sources out there in the world come in a wide variety of modalities, and students need to be able to comprehend and create them, using reading, writing, listening, speaking, viewing, and creating skills.

- Using a variety of sources for social studies instruction provides access and opportunity for students to collect information, try to make sense of it, and, potentially, create new knowledge or understandings to share with others. It also prepares students for the wide variety of forms in which information exists in the outside world.
- The best questions come out of authentic interest and from invested questioners.
- Embrace the possibilities associated with social studies instruction!

Index

Note: Tables, Figures, and Illustrations are indicated by italicized page references.

Abdelrahman, M. S. H. B., 14
accessibility, 90, 137, 138
active listening, 71
active readers, 13
Active View of Reading, 11, 12, *12*, 13
Adobe, 136
advocacy, writing for, 32
Afflerbach, P., 14
All the Way to America (Yaccarino), 77
alternate sources, for inquiry, 138
American Revolution, 114
analysis, of sources, 92, 93, 95
Analyzing Maps, Teacher's Guide, 120–21
anchor chart, *16*, 19, 92; of Children Just Like Me, *96*; sentence frames in, 55, 56–57; for speaking, 52; speaking skills in, *60*
Angel Island, Immigrant Station Foundation, Immigrant Voices (website), 77
"Applying Disciplinary Tools and Concepts," 106, 111
argument summaries, 91, 97
attention: listening relation to, 70, 71; multimodal communication relation to, 103
audience: multimodal creation relation to, 87, 97; scaffolding for, 98; writing relation to, 31, 32
audio: listening to, 76; of written texts, 70, 71
auditory sources, 93

background knowledge, 12–13
backing claims, evidence for, 51
Battle of Bunkers Hill, bird's-eye-view maps of, *113*
Battle of Long Island, panoramic maps of, 116, *116*
belief systems, 26
Benefits and Costs Graphic Organizer, *137*, *143*
The Big List of Classroom Discussion Strategies (Gonzalez), 57, 62
bird's-eye-view maps, 107, *108*, 109; of Battle of Bunkers Hill, *113*; of *The New York Campaign*, 114
Black Ants and Buddhists (Cowhey), 57
book pass, 9, 11
brainstorming, 32, 85, 86, *86*; drafting and, 98; inquiry and, 130
Brittanica Kids (online encyclopedia), *132*
Bsharah, M. S., 14
bubble graphic organizer, 67–68, *68*
bundle, bullet, and view, 80, *80*

C3 Framework. *See College, Career, and Civic Life (C3) Framework for Social Studies State Standards*
C3 Teachers, Inquiries Archive, 127
canonical elements, 105
Canva, 136
cartographer, 109
character development, 90

chat and change topics: for inquiry, 139; for listening, 81; for multimodal creation, 100; for reading, 27; for speaking, 63; for viewing, 117–18; for writing, 44
Children Just Like Me, 94, 96
choice board, 98, *99*
civic engagement, 98, 125, 138
civic participation: communication and, 85; listening relation to, 70; speaking and, 49
civics, K-2 lessons for, 74
civil discourse, 48
class discussion, 11; norms for, 48; for prewriting, 40; in research-based instructional practice, 36–37
Classroom Materials at the Library of Congress, 21, 26, 77, 117
classroom resources, for sight words, 35
co-construction, of meaning, 54
collaboration: in discussion, 58–59; listening relation to, 70; in speaking, 48
collaborative conversations, 53
College, Career, and Civic Life (C3) Framework for Social Studies State Standards, 5, 39; "Applying Disciplinary Tools and Concepts," 106, 111; critical reading in, 21–22; Inquiry Arc, *125*, 127; K-2 civics lessons in, 74; listening in, 72, 78; multimodal creation and, 91; reading in, 14–15; speaking in, 52, 58; writing in, 35
color-coded reference, for T-chart, 75
combined graphic organizer, *25*
Common Core State Standards for English Language Arts, 5; informational texts in, 111–12; listening in, 72, 78; maps in, 106–7; multimodal creation and, 91–92; reading and, 15, 22; speaking in, 52–53, 54, 58–59; writing in, 35, 39–40, 97
communication: of ideas, 85, 86–87, 90, 95; of meaning, 91; multimodal, 87–88, 103; speaking as, 48; writing as, 33, 35, 39
community-based research, 98
compelling questions, *79*, 127
competencies, disciplinary literacy and, 58
comprehension, 51; of informational texts, 112; listening, 70, 71; of maps, 113; speaking and, 53; of written texts, 104. *See also* reading comprehension
content-area literacy, 1, 4

content-area vocabulary, sentence frames for, 50
content-based arguments, 51
content creators, 90
contour maps, 107, *108*, 109, *115*
control, mentor texts relation to, 90
controversial topics, 48, 50
creation: as communication, 87–88; mentor texts and, 90; multimodal, 87, 90, 91–92, 97, 100; research-based instructional practice for, 98, *99*; speaking compared to, 48
creation resources: for K-2 lessons, 95; for 3-5 lessons, *99*, 100
critical conversations, 105
critical inquiry, 123
critical reading, in *C3 Framework*, 21–22
critical thinking, 104, 125
The Curator Chat Series (short videos), 95

Dalton, B., 88
Deadly Aim (Walker), *10*
decoding, 17
Dewey, John, 123
digital technologies, 58, 91, 97
disciplinary literacy: competencies and, 58; content-area literacy compared to, 4
discussion: class, 11, 36–37, 40, 48; inquiry relation to, 124; listening in, 69; pyramid, 60–61; questions in, 78; rules for, 53, 58–59; scaffolding for, 51; sentence frames for, 50; understanding relation to, 56, 78. *See also* class discussion
drafting, 34, 37; brainstorming and, 98; in K-2 lessons, 34; for sharing, 43. *See also* prewriting
drawings, 88

ecological literacy, 3
editing, 34
electronic resources, 17. *See also* technology supports
elementary school, schedule in, 2
English language arts, 2, 5
environmental print, 92
Essential Instructional Practices in Early Literacy, 38
Essential Practices in Literacy, 44
The *Everybody* Series (Dooley), 132

evidence: for backing claims, 51; in inquiry-based practices, 126
evidence-based argumentation skills, 104
exemplar lessons, 5
expectations: for class discussion, 48; for listening, 61, 81; for speaking, 61
Explore (audio tours), *99*
Extending Interactive Writing into Grades 2-5 (Roth & Dabrowski), 38
Eyewitness Presidents (DK Children), 76

factual information, in opinion writing, 39
fifth-grade students, 9
Finding Primary Sources, Library of Congress, 21, 26, 117
Finding Stuff Out (video), 132
first-grade students, 31
504 plan, 5
Focused Inquiry, 127, *128*, 129, *142*
Follow that Map! (Ritchie), 110
Forever Ago (podcast), 95
form, function relation to, 87
formative performance tasks, 130
Forty Maps That Explain Food in America (Klein & Locke), 138
four-square organizer, with prompts, *41*
fourth-grade students, 67, 85, 86–87, 103
framing, for discussion, 51
Frankel, Katherine, 3
From Mapping Sam (Hesselberth), 98, *99*
"From 'What Is Reading?' to What Is Literacy?," 3
Frozen Secrets (Walker), *10*
frustration, 81
function, form relation to, 87

genre, 21
geography indicators, 106, 111
goals, speaking for, 52
Google Earth Education, 117
Google Geo Tools, 110
Google search, 130, 136
Grandfather's Journey (Say), 77
Grant, S. G., 127
graphical devices, 103, 104, 105, 106–7, 110–11, 117
Graphical Rating Tool, *105*, 106

graphic organizer, 9, *24*; Benefits and Costs, *137*, *143*; bubble, 67–68, *68*; combined, *25*; for guiding questions, 23; inquiry and, 135; for listening, 79, 80; for prewriting, 40, *41*, 42, *42*, 43; questions in, 23, 24; in research-based instructional practice, 19–20; for written summarization, 34
Great Lakes region, 22–23
grouping routines, 18
guided inquiry, 123
guiding questions, 23
"Guiding Students to Develop Multimodal Literacy," 100

Harmer, 23
Hesselberth, Joyce, 98
highlighting tools, 18
high school, 2
high-stakes testing, 2
high-stakes topics, 48
historians, 23, 25, 81
historical literacy, 3
Home Then and Now (Nelson), 19
How to Make an Apple Pie and See the World (Priceman), 129

idea curation, for writing, 32
ideas, 5, 78, 85, 86–87, 90, 95
IDM. *See* Inquiry Design Model
IEPs. *See* individualized education programs
"I Heard" statements, 74–75
illustrations, 88
Immigration (C3 Teachers), 77
Immigration Challenges for New Americans (Library of Congress), 77
Immigration/Push and Pull Factors (website), 77
independence, 145
independent composition, 97
independent readers, 12
Indigenous people, 22, 23
individualized education programs (IEPs), 5
inferences, 24
infographic, 136
informational texts, 92, 111–12
informational writing, 35, 39
"Information Book Read-Alouds as Models for Second-Grade Authors," 95

informed citizenry, 12, 26
inquiry, 125–26, 128, 145; alternate sources for, 138; chat and change topics for, 139; critical, 123; Focused, 127, *128*, 129, *142*; questions relation to, 124, 127, 130; sharing of, 129; supporting questions for, 130, 135, 136–37
Inquiry Arc, *125*, 127
Inquiry-Based Practice in Social Studies Education (Grant, Swan, & Lee), 138
inquiry-based practices, 123, 138; evidence in, 126; listening relation to, 70, 72; questions in, 2, 26, 61–62
Inquiry Design Model (IDM), 127, 133, *133–34, 141*
inquiry resources, 132
instructional content, state-specific content relation to, 22
instructional decisions, 126
instructional strategies, 5
intention, listening relation to, 69
The Interactive Constitution (Miles & Pinilla), 95
interactive writing, 34, 36
interdisciplinary instruction, 1, 2
interdisciplinary skills, 138
interpersonal skills, for speaking, 48
interpretation: of graphical devices, 106; of informational texts, 111–12; of maps, 117
interviews, 67, 69
introductions, questions for, 47–48
iterative process, writing as, 33
"I Think" statements, 74–75

joint composition, 34

K-2 lessons, 107; for civics, 74; creation resources for, 95; Focused Inquiry in, *128*, 129; inquiry resources for, 132; listening resources for, 76; multimodal creation in, 91–92; prewriting in, 34; reading resources for, 21; sample texts for, 17; speaking resources for, 57; on viewing, 108–10; viewing resources for, 110; writing in, 35–36; writing resources for, 38
K-3 Essential 6, Bullet 1, 38
keywords, 23

Kids Discover, Regions of North America (magazine), 43
Kid's Talk, Stories of Refugee Children (documentary), 77
King, Martin Luther, Jr., *89*
knowledge: prior, 14, 18, 19, 51; professional, 126; reading relation to, 12–13; sharing of, 100; social construction of, 49

language arts, 13
language goals, 5
learning disabilities, reading comprehension relation to, 13
Lee, J., 127
lesson application, 97
lesson ideas, 5
Library of Congress, 19, 113–15; *Classroom Materials at the*, 21, 26, 77, 117; *Maps from the World Digital Library*, 110
listening, 52–53; to audio, 76; expectations for, 61, 81; reading compared to, 69–70; as reciprocal processes, 54; research-based instructional practice for, 74–75, 79, 81; speaking relation to, 71, 72; 3-5 lessons on, 78–79. *See also* speaking
listening resources: for K-2 lessons, 76; for 3-5 lessons, 77
literacy. *See specific topics*
Long Island, New York and Staten Island, contour maps of, *115*
Looking with Lavar (Burton), *99*
low-stakes topics, 48

main ideas, 78
Making Classroom Discussions Work (Lo), 62
Mapping Penny's World (Leedy), *99*, 110
maps, 106, *108, 113, 114, 115, 116*; comprehension of, 113; interpretation of, 117; in K-2 lessons, 107, 108–9; research-based instructional practice on, 117; in 3-5 lessons, 110–11, 112, 113
Maps (Mizielinska & Mizielinski), 110
Maps from the World Digital Library, 110
meaning, 4; co-construction of, 54; communication of, 91; listening relation to, 69; reading comprehension relation to, 11; reading for, 26; in visual elements, 104; writing relation to, 32

meaning-based reading skills, 15
media literacy, 3
memory, listening relation to, 70
mentor texts, 90, 92, 93, 95, 100
Michigan Agricultural Facts & Figures, *131*, 132
Michigan History for Kids, 25
middle school, 2
Migrant Child Storytelling (website), 77
misconceptions, 75
modeling: accessibility relation to, 90; of prewriting, 31–32, 37–38; in research-based instructional practice, 19–20; of sentence frames, 50
monitoring, scanning relation to, 14
multilingual learners, sentence frames for, 50
multimodal communication, 87–88, 103
multimodal creation, 87, 100; in K-2 lessons, 91–92; scaffolding of, 90; 3-5 lessons on, 97
multimodal literacy, 3–4, *100*, 138, 145
multimodal sources, 76
Nathan Hale's Hazardous Tales (Hale), 117
National Archives Analysis Tools, 110
National Council for the Social Studies (NCSS), 2, 124
National Geographic Classroom Map, 110
National Geographic Kids, U.S. States and Territories (website), 26, 43
National Geographic Regions (website), 44
Native Knowledge 360 (website), 26
navigation, 107
NCSS. *See* National Council for the Social Studies
Nelson, R., 19
New London Group, 87
Newsela (online collection), 62
The New York Campaign, bird's-eye-view maps of, *114*
nonfiction, 11
norms, for class discussion, 48
note taking, scanning and, 24

observe prompts, 113
Ojibwa people, 22, 23
online creations, 87
opinion writing, 39–40
oral technologies, 58, 91
organization, of ideas, 90

Ottawa people, 22, 23

panoramic maps, 112, 116, *116*
paraphrasing, 78
passive decoding, 13
passive listening, 71
perspective taking, 51
Philosophical Dialogue, 51
photographs, 88
Pictionary (game), 80
points of view, in sources, 79
Potawatomi people, 22, 23
The President (C3 Teachers), 76
President of the United States (online article), 76
Pressley, M., 14
previewing skills, 22–23, 25
prewriting, 34, 36; graphic organizer for, 40, *41*, 42, *42*, 43; in K-2 lessons, 34; modeling of, 31–32, 37–38; questions in, 39
Priceman, Marjorie, 129
primary sources, listening relation to, 70
print technology, 91, 97
prior knowledge: QAR and, 51; reading comprehension relation to, 14; in research-based instructional practice, 18, 19
process writing, 36
professional development, 123
professional knowledge, 126
professional learning communities (PLCs). *See* chat and change topics
"Projects That Have Been Put to the Test," 57
prompts, 113, 115–16; four-square organizer with, *41*; for introductions, 47–48; prewriting relation to, 40; for speaking, 54
publishing, 34
pyramid discussion, 60–61

Question-Answer Relationships (QAR), 15–16, 21, 51
Questioning the Author (QtA), 51
questions, 16, 17; compelling, *79*, 127; in discussion, 78; in inquiry-based practices, 2, 26, 61–62; inquiry relation to, 124, 127, 130; for introductions, 47–48; in prewriting, 39; for reading

comprehension, 13–14, 18, 51; in research-based instructional practice, 20–21, 23; in research-based pedagogy, 50–51; scanning and, 24, 25; supporting, 67–68, 69, 72, 73, 74–75, 130, 135, 136–37; for understanding, 58; young children and, 15
"Questions, Tasks, Sources," 132
questions prompts, 113

racial literacy, 3
reading, 81; Active View of, 11, 12, *12*, 13; in *C3 Framework*, 14–15; chat and change topics for, 27; critical, 21–22; listening compared to, 69–70; for meaning, 26; previewing skills for, 22–23; skimming and, 9, 11; viewing compared to, 117; writing relation to, 32
reading comprehension, 11, 13–14, 18, 51, 71
reading resources: for K-2 lessons, 21; for 3-5 lessons, *25*, 26
Real Classrooms, Real Teachers (Brugar & Roberts), 138
reciprocal processes, 49, 54
recordings, 88
Reflective Discussion Circles, 51
reflect prompts, 113
research-based instructional practice, 18; class discussion in, 36–37; for creation, 98, 99; for listening, 74–75, 79, 81; on maps, 115–16; on mentor texts, 92, 93, 95; modeling in, 19–20; previewing skills in, 23; pyramid discussion as, 61; questions in, 20–21, 23; for speaking, 54, 55, 56; for viewing, 109; for writing, 36–37, 40, 41
research-based pedagogy: questions in, 50–51; sentence frames in, 49–50
Research Notes Organizer, 18–19
revision, 34
Revolution of Ideas (Swan), 132
rote memorization, 2
rules, for discussion, 53, 58–59
running text, 88, 103

sample texts, for K-2 lessons, 17
scaffolding, 16; for audience, 98; for discussion, 51; inquiry relation to, 124, 126; of multimodal creation, 90; for writing, 39
scanning: as previewing skill, 22–23, 25; questions and, 24, 25; for reading comprehension, 13, 14
schedule, in elementary school, 2
"School Lunch, Supper Menus Saturday," *136*
scientific research, on reading, 11
self-questioning, 13
sentence frames, 54, 55, 57; in anchor chart, *55*, 56–57; in research-based pedagogy, 49–50
"Sentence Frames and Sentence Starters," 57
sharing: drafting for, 43; of inquiry, 129; of knowledge, 100; in research-based instructional practice, 21; speaking and, 49; of thinking, 56–57
sight words, classroom resources for, 35
signed language, 48, 69
Singer, Allison, 72, 74
skimming, 9, 11; as previewing skill, 22–23; for reading comprehension, 13, 14
small-group inquiry models, 123
social construction, of knowledge, 49
socialization, writing relation to, 44
social justice, reading relation to, 26
social studies. *See specific topics*
Socratic seminars, 52
sources, 25, 70; alternate, 138; analysis of, 92, 93, 95; multimodal, 76; points of view in, 79
Source Suggestions, *93*
speaking, 58, 70; chat and change topics for, 63; civic participation and, 49; comprehension and, 53; expectations for, 61; for goals, 52; listening relation to, 71, 72; research-based instructional practice for, 54, 55, 56; 3-5 lessons and, 59, 60; writing compared to, 48
Speaking and Listening in Content Area Learning (online collection), 57, 62, 77
speaking opportunities, supports in, 63
speaking resources: for K-2 lessons, 57; for 3-5 lessons, 62
speaking skills, in anchor chart, *60*
"Staging the Inquiry," 127
stamina, for writing, 37
standardized test reports, 88–89

State Department of Agriculture, 130
State Historical Society Websites, 25
state-specific content, instructional content relation to, 22
strategic readers, 13
strategies, for reading comprehension, 13–14
student voice, 145
summarization: inquiry relation to, 124; of written text, 78
summative performance tasks, 132
supporting details, 78
supporting questions, 67–68, 69, 72; for inquiry, 130, 135, 136–37; T-chart for, 73, 74–75
supports: in speaking opportunities, 63; for writing, 37, 39
Swan, K., 127

T-chart, 54, *73*; inquiry and, 135; for supporting questions, 73, 74–75
Teacher's Guide (Library of Congress), 113–15, *120–21*
teaching and learning cycle, *90*, 97
Teaching and Learning Cycle (Victoria State Government), 95
technology supports, 15, 17, 18
text-to-speech technology, 17, 18
thinking: critical, 104, 125; graphic organizer relation to, 42; sharing of, 56–57; writing relation to, 33
think-pair-share, 52
third-grade students, 61
Those Shoes (Boelts), 38
3-5 lessons: creation resources for, *99*, 100; on graphical devices, 110–11; IDM in, 133, *133–34*; on listening, 78–79; listening resources for, 77; maps in, 110–11, 112; on multimodal creation, 97; reading resources for, *25*, *26*; speaking and, 59, 60; speaking resources for, 62; viewing resources for, 117; writing and, 39–40; writing resources for, 43–44
Time for Kids (online magazine), 57
A True Book (Rau), 26, 43
Try It! (Caplan), 134, 135

Ultimate Food Atlas (Castalado & Mihaly), 138

Underground Fire (Walker), *10*
understanding, 1, 75; discussion relation to, 56, 78; listening relation to, 72; questions for, 58; reading for, 12
United States Department of Agriculture, Food Access Resource Atlas (online resource), 138
Urban Farmer, 130
"Using Choice Boards for Student Engagement," *100*
Using QR Codes to Share (website), *100*

verbalization, 47–48
verbal protocols, 14
viewing, 103–4; chat and change topics for, 117–18; K-2 lessons on, 108–10; reading compared to, 117. *See also* graphical devices; maps
viewing resources: for K-2 lessons, 110; for 3-5 lessons, 117
visual elements, meaning in, 104
visual literacy, 4
Visual Thinking Strategies (VTS), 104–5, 109, 136
vocabulary learning, 71
VTS. *See* Visual Thinking Strategies

Walker, Sally M., *10*, 11
Wants and Needs Collection (Korenek), 38
web-based resources, 130
What Does the President Do?, 76
"What School Lunch Looked Like Each Decade Since 1900," 138
What's the President's Job? (Singer), 72, 74, 76
What the World Eats (D'Auision & Menzel), 138
Why Did People (Im)migrate?, 83
word choice, 90
The World That Feeds Us (Castalado), 138
writing, 31, 34, 90; chat and change topics for, 44; in *Common Core State Standards for English Language Arts*, 35, 39–40, 97; as communication, 33, 35, 39; listening compared to, 81; literacy relation to, 4; reading relation to, 32; research-based instructional practice for, 36–37, 40, 41; socialization relation to, 44; speaking compared to, 48. *See also* prewriting

writing process, 33, 34
writing resources: for K-2 lessons, 38; for 3-5 lessons, 43–44
The Writing Strategies Book (Serravallo), 38, 44
Written in Bone (Walker), *10*

written summarization, graphic organizer for, 34
written texts: audio of, 70, 71; comprehension of, 104; summarization of, 78

young children, 14, 15

About the Authors

Kathryn L. Roberts is a professor of reading, language, and literature in the Division of Teacher Education at Wayne State University in Detroit, Michigan. A former elementary teacher, Roberts earned her PhD in curriculum, teaching, and educational policy from Michigan State University. She now teaches undergraduate and graduate courses in literacy education and enjoys working with educators through professional development. Her research focuses on content-area literacy, visual literacy, early and emergent literacy, and reading comprehension. Her work can be found in journals, such as *The Elementary School Journal*, *The Reading Teacher*, *The Journal of Social Studies Research*, and *The Journal of Teacher Education*.

Kristy A. Brugar is a professor of social studies education, the chair of the Instructional Leadership and Academic Curriculum Department (ILAC), and the Robert L. and Nan A. Huddleston Presidential Professor of Education at the University of Oklahoma. Brugar has served as the chair of the board of directors for the National Council for History Education (2020–2022), a professional organization that elevates the importance of teaching through professional learning, community building, and advocacy. Brugar earned her PhD in curriculum, instruction, and teacher education from Michigan State University. Her research focuses on teacher development, social studies/history education, and interdisciplinary instruction involving inquiry, social studies, literacy, and visual arts. She has published articles in *The Elementary School Journal*, *The Journal of Social Studies Research*, and *The Journal of Teacher Education*.

www.ingramcontent.com/pod-product-compliance
Lightning Source LLC
Chambersburg PA
CBHW080635230426
43663CB00016B/2883